RAND

How Do Education and Training Affect a Country's Economic Performance? A Literature Survey

Roland Sturm

Supported by the
Lilly Endowment Inc.

**Institute on
Education and Training**

RAND's Institute on Education and Training conducts policy analysis to help improve education and training for all Americans.

The Institute examines *all* forms of education and training that people may get during their lives. These include formal schooling from preschool through college; employer-provided training (civilian and military); postgraduate education; proprietary trade schools; and the informal learning that occurs in families, in communities, and with exposure to the media. Reexamining the field's most basic premises, the Institute goes beyond the narrow concerns of each component to view the education and training enterprise as a whole. It pays special attention to how the parts of the enterprise affect one another and how they are shaped by the larger environment. The Institute

- Examines the performance of the education and training system

- Analyzes problems and issues raised by economic, demographic, and national security trends

- Evaluates the impact of policies on broad, system-wide concerns

- Helps decisionmakers formulate and implement effective solutions.

To ensure that its research affects policy and practice, the Institute conducts outreach and disseminates findings to policymakers, educators, researchers, and the public. It also trains policy analysts in the field of education.

RAND is a private, nonprofit institution, incorporated in 1948, which engages in nonpartisan research and analysis on problems of national security and the public welfare. The Institute builds on RAND's long tradition—interdisciplinary, empirical research held to the highest standards of quality, objectivity, and independence.

PREFACE

This report reviews research on the role of education and training in economic performance. It focuses on the long-run and international perspective of economic trends and education to counteract the fairly myopic view of economic conditions encountered in many policy debates. In addition to surveying research on the relationships between education and training and the macroeconomic phenomenon of economic growth and individual wages, this review discusses alternative approaches that take a more systems-oriented approach than the standard economic framework.

This research was sponsored by RAND's Institute on Education and Training with funds from a grant by the Lilly Endowment, Inc. The Institute on Education and Training conducts policy analysis to help improve education and training for all Americans.

CONTENTS

FIGURES AND TABLES

Figure

Table

SUMMARY

In policy debates, the U.S. education and training system is often blamed for our eroding position in the world economy. Many claim that dramatic changes are necessary to avoid an economic decline, or that improving an inefficient education and training system will produce a high payoff. To help decisionmakers assess such claims, this report reviews the economic literature linking education and training to economic performance.

In brief, we find that U.S. economic performance is much more competitive than policy debates often assume, that education and training are clearly connected to economic performance, but that the major economic theories attempting to describe this connection all have important flaws. As a result, crucial questions for education policy remain unanswered. Less-orthodox economic frameworks may be able to answer these questions but must first be substantially refined.

ASSESSING U.S. COMPETITIVENESS

It is widely believed that the United States is losing its industrial core compared to other advanced countries like Japan and Germany. But long-run, international analysis reveals that there is little evidence of de-industrialization or of falling labor productivity. There can be no doubt, however, that other industrial countries have caught up. Specifically:

- The United States *has* recently experienced lower growth rates in gross domestic product (GDP), labor productivity, and total factor productivity growth (changes in productivity after adjusting for changes in all inputs) than many of its competitors.

- But the U.S. share of manufacturing output in the OECD, like Japan's, has increased, whereas the share of Germany and other OECD countries has dropped.

- The United States *has* experienced a general decline in its share of world trade. But whereas the U.S. share of OECD exports—in contrast to total manufacturing—has become smaller overall, high-technology industries fared better.

- In terms of real GDP per capita, the relative position of the United States *has* declined from 40 percent above the OECD mean in 1971 to 25 percent above that mean in 1991, but the United States remains the world leader.

- Labor productivity *has* grown more slowly in the United States than in other countries over the last 40 years—but faster in the preceding 70 years. Long-run data suggest that all industrial countries experienced a productivity slowdown in the 1970s and that this general slowdown indicated a return to normal growth rates at the end of an unusually fast growth period.

- Other countries, in particular Japan and the nations of Western Europe, are not quickly surpassing the United States but rather approach the U.S. level of per capita GDP and labor productivity as part of a general convergence trend among OECD countries. This convergence is possible because these countries improved their social capability to exploit the "advantages of backwardness." Economists believe that education played an important part in this improvement.

- Although labor productivity is a good indicator of economic welfare, changes in labor productivity do not directly measure labor's contribution to economic growth.

- In general, the trade-as-war metaphor is concerned with the potential loss of world economic leadership. But although economic leadership may contribute to national pride, political power, or military strength, it is an indicator of only relative, not absolute, economic welfare.

In summary, current findings may not be reassuring about the *relative* U.S. position and do not provide guarantees for the future. But the economic data do not support widely repeated claims of deindustrialization or productivity loss—nor do they necessarily suggest a need for dramatic and instantaneous changes in education and training.

LINKING EDUCATION TO ECONOMIC PERFORMANCE

Education and training are clearly connected to economic performance. Regardless of the particular method used to measure this contribution, education and its effects on labor quality are generally found to be among the most important contributors to economic growth. For example, data show that countries with comparable levels of education are converging among themselves, *but they do not close the gap to countries with higher educational levels.*

And even though the data show convergence and not that the United States is quickly being surpassed by other countries, it is important to consider factors that may allow countries to gain comparative advantage in certain industries. The relative U.S. performance in high-technology industries has been good in the past few decades, but this competitive position may not hold in the future, since government policies may create comparative advantages (or disadvantages). Education and training policies are one leading candidate to do so.

So far, attempts to describe and quantify precisely how the education and training system influences economic performance—and thus to understand which related policies might have the greatest economic value—have not yet succeeded. (Likewise, the importance of human resources to a firm's success has been touted in much of the popular business literature, but the overall evidence is sketchy.) Most such attempts can be grouped into two approaches—one focusing on the macroeconomic phenomenon of economic growth, the other one analyzing the effect of education and training on individual wages and (to a lesser extent) on worker productivity.

Growth Accounting

Economists have tried to measure the sources of economic growth by analyzing changes in the quality of labor and capital, changes in the economic and policy environment, and technical progress. This approach, known as growth accounting, was spurred by the realization that the growth of real income per capita over the last century cannot be explained by capital accumulation or more labor input alone. It has provided some of the most-cited estimates of education's role in economic growth.

Growth accounting can be useful for international comparisons. *Such estimates show that the lower growth rates in the United States compared to other countries cannot be ascribed to smaller increases in formal education or labor quality.* An investigation into the large variance across countries in the estimated role of education and economic growth could provide major new insights, but such work has not yet been done. For example, growth accounting estimates show the role of labor quality improvement in German economic growth to be very small. Could this be explained by training and other forms of education which are excluded from standard growth accounting calculations?

Though growth accounting is a useful and widely accepted framework, it is quite narrow and even the researchers citing growth accounting estimates are not always aware of its limitations. Growth accounting, for example, ignores important interactions between different causes of growth, such as the link between technical progress and capital growth. In particular, the demand for investment depends on the opportunity for the introduction of new technology; recent technological progress in computers, for example, has stimulated large investments in information technology. In addition, the measurement of education and training is incomplete and largely limited to years of formal education. Thus, the scope and reliability of widely cited growth accounting estimates are often misunderstood.

Wage and Productivity Analyses

The positive correlation between education/training and wages/income has stimulated many attempts to establish a causal connection at the microeconomic level. Human capital theory, which dominates this literature, considers education as an investment that makes individuals more productive. Its major competing framework, the screening hypothesis, argues that education does not actually improve an individual's productivity, but serves rather as a sorting mechanism that distinguishes inherently more-productive from less-productive individuals and assigns them to occupations. Under both models, higher wages for more-educated workers are feasible only if these workers are more productive. The two theories are also similar insofar as correlations between income, productivity, and education are concerned. Thus, there are no convincing tests to distinguish between them using observational data.

Like growth accounting models, the microstudies of the effect of education and training on productivity have limited value for policymakers who must respond to a changing environment. Recent research by Baumol (1990) and Murphy, Shleifer, and Vishny (1991) draws our attention to the importance of the gap between private and social returns to education and its role in economic growth. For example, economies with a high proportion of engineering students grow faster than economies with a high proportion of lawyers. But most previous research has focused on the private returns to education and training. Though these can be estimated fairly easily from earnings data, they are less important for educational planning than the social returns. These latter estimates should include estimates of social benefits and costs that accrue to persons other than the individual educated—but almost invariably do not. Because the social rates of return to education in traditional research are inadequately formulated, such findings provide little guidance for policymakers.

UNCONVENTIONAL APPROACHES

Overall, these two conventional approaches are not well suited to analyzing the current policy issues of international competitiveness and technological change. The less-orthodox literature in the history of economic development and the economics of technological change may provide a new "vehicle" to analyze the role of education and training. Two theoretical approaches are important: transaction cost theory and evolutionary economic theory. These alternatives take a more systems-oriented approach, although they have yet to be applied to education and training. For example, economic studies of technological change show that differences in productivity growth across firms and industries can be explained in substantial part by R&D spending. (The connection between R&D and education and training may be closer than it appears at first sight; some studies suggest that R&D expenditures measure to a large extent "training" costs for the research staff.)

Unfortunately, these lines of research are not unified by a complete theoretical framework; they include approaches as diverse as business and economic history, evolutionary economics, and case studies of matched firms in different countries. And such research so far has largely been limited to the most educated part of the workforce. An important exception is the work in matched firm comparisons conducted by Prais et al. (1989)—an approach that is currently extended to the United States in joint research with RAND. Expanding and testing these alternative approaches could address several of the central features of economic growth that have been ignored in the existing literature on education and training's contribution to productivity. A number of hypotheses might be explored: Are education and training levels higher in concentrated industries? Are industries with higher education and training levels experiencing faster productivity growth? Are education and training levels related to firm size?

Clearly, economic guidance for policy on education and training needs further development. Though far from perfect, these less-orthodox frameworks seem to offer the most promising approach.

ACKNOWLEDGMENTS

David Finegold and Bob Schoeni carefully reviewed an earlier draft and made detailed suggestions, which substantially changed and improved this report. Earlier discussions with John Strauss and Steve Carroll are also gratefully acknowledged. Mitchell Wade wrote the first draft of the summary.

Chapter One

INTRODUCTION

Policy discussions of the international competitiveness of U.S. firms almost invariably turn to the education and training system as a prime suspect for the eroding U.S. position in the world economy. Reports by the Office of Technology Assessment (1990), the Commission on the Skills of the American Workforce (1990), and many others point to weaknesses in the organization of the education and training (ET) system in the United States and claim that dramatic changes are necessary to avoid an economic decline. ET is generally perceived to be a central factor in determining a country's economic performance and improving an inefficient ET system may have high payoffs. Inadequate ET is linked to declining international competitiveness in high-quality goods and services, thus eroding the higher U.S. living standards relative to other countries. Often the stronger claim is made that a weak ET system leads to a deterioration in living standards in absolute terms, not just relative to other countries.

The recent wave of policy studies is largely concerned with the organization of the ET system and therefore does not provide a more complete discussion of macroeconomic trends and the world economy. Chapter Two surveys recent economic analyses, provides relevant statistics, and discusses different interpretations of the productivity data. It may be of particular interest to researchers of the ET system because its international comparison and the long-run perspective are not typically found in the current policy debate. Chapters Three through Five then discuss three strategies that have been or should be employed to analyze the relationship between ET and economic performance: the contribution of ET to macroeconomic growth, the effect of ET on an individual's productivity (measured by

1

wages or directly), and the link between ET (or "knowledge") and technological change.

Macroeconomic research of the contribution of ET to economic growth (Chapter Three) began when economists realized that the growth of real income per capita over the last century cannot be explained by capital accumulation or more labor input alone (Solow, 1957; Kendrick, 1961; Denison, 1962). Economists have tried since then to measure the sources of economic growth by analyzing changes in the quality of labor and capital, changes in the economic and policy environment, and technical progress. The so-called growth accounting framework has been the main approach and the often-cited numbers measuring education's contribution to economic growth come out of this literature.

At the microeconomic (individual) level, the almost universal positive correlation between education and income has also stimulated many attempts to establish a causal connection between ET and productivity (Chapter Four). Human capital theory, founded by T. W. Schultz (1961, 1963), Becker (1962, 1964), and Mincer (1962, 1974), soon became the dominating approach and also underlies many of the macroeconomic estimates since Denison (1962). In fact, *The New Palgrave. A Dictionary of Economics* (Eatwell, Milgate, and Newman, 1987), a standard reference work on economics, refers the reader looking for "Economics of Education" to "Human Capital." The human capital framework has been employed to estimate the economic returns to education in many countries and to study several of the central questions in educational planning using micro data: how earning structures depend on the educational systems, the connection between education and migration, the efficiency of the educational system, and the returns on investment in education versus physical capital. However, human capital theory is only one of several theories capable of explaining empirical regularities, and theories based on different assumptions about the effect of ET on productivity can have dramatically different implications for educational policies.

In contrast to the mainstream macro- and microeconomic analysis discussed in Chapters Three and Four, research on technological change focuses on the organizational level of the firm and the development of industries and remains a relatively neglected field.

Chapter Five argues that some of the most crucial questions surrounding the ET debate may be best analyzed in the more heterodox frameworks found in this literature: Except for simple production technologies, such as agriculture in developing countries, the relationship of ET, productivity, and technical change cannot be studied for an individual (or family) in isolation. The creation and use of new knowledge, innovation, and diffusion of new technologies require individuals working together. However, economic studies built on a neoclassical foundation like human capital theory focus on individual decisions and assume that interactions are governed through more or less functioning markets, the "invisible hand." But economic historians espouse the opposite point of view: Business organizations and their supporting institutions have shaped markets, economic development, and the competitiveness of nations (Chandler, 1990). These factors may be essential to understanding the issues of productivity growth and competitiveness and it may be necessary to focus more on the complexity of social systems than on markets. Unfortunately, the research discussed in Chapter Five is not unified by a complete theoretical framework and includes approaches as diverse as business and economic history, evolutionary economics, and case studies of matched firms in different countries.

There have been several other reviews of the relationship between education and productivity (Dean, 1984; Kazis, 1988; Rasell and Appelbaum, 1992). Dean collects a number of specific research papers on education and productivity, mentioned in Chapters Three and Four, but without connecting the very different approaches taken by different authors. Kazis (1988) and Rasell and Appelbaum (1992) provide surveys similar to the one in this report, although each one has a different focus: Kazis analyzes the implications for U.S. manufacturing and educational reform, Rasell and Appelbaum consider prenatal care, early childhood education, and medical care. In contrast, this report discusses economic trends (Chapter Two) and nonstandard economic approaches (Chapter Five).

PRODUCTIVITY AND COMPETITIVENESS: WHAT DO THE DATA SHOW?

The United States has recently experienced lower growth rates in GDP, labor productivity, and total factor productivity growth (changes in productivity after adjusting for changes in all input) than many of its competitors. Understandably, this has caused much concern about international competitiveness and whether the United States can ". . . mount a more energetic and successful response to the challenge of newly rising foreign competitors after 1970 than Britain did after 1870" (Abramowitz, 1981). Changing an educational system has long-run effects and it is important to see actual economic trends in a similar perspective. Because policy discussions rarely offer such a long-run view, this chapter provides a more in-depth discussion of international economic developments.

WHAT IS PRODUCTIVITY AND COMPETITIVENESS?

The basic idea of productivity is straightforward: It is the ratio of outputs to inputs. The most commonly reported partial productivity index (because it refers only to one class of inputs) is labor productivity, defined as output per unit of labor input (worker or work hour). Gross domestic product (GDP) is an easily available output statistic, but many other refinements have been made. Without population growth and changes in labor market participation and annual work hours, there is a constant linear relationship between labor productivity and GDP per capita. Thus, labor productivity and GDP per capita are two closely related measures of economic welfare.

5

Table 2.1 reports real GDP per capita relative to the OECD average of 25 industrialized countries. Even though the relative position of the United States has declined—from 40 percent above the OECD mean in 1971 to 25 percent above the mean in 1991—and there has been a general convergence among OECD countries, the United States remains the leader in terms of real GDP per capita. In the popular press, one finds the occasional claim that per capita GDP is higher in Japan, but such calculations are based on current exchange rates and current exchange rates are not useful to compare economic welfare. The value of the German mark, for example, has doubled between 1985 and 1992, but nobody would claim that the German standard of living has doubled during this period. Under current exchange rates, many goods and services are more expensive in Japan or Germany than in the United States and consumers get less for their money than they would here. A better comparison of per capita income is therefore based on purchasing power parities (PPPs).

Labor productivity or GDP per capita is often reported as the rate of change of an index number, for example, as the growth (or decline) in labor productivity, rather than as a level. Table 2.2 presents the labor productivity growth rates from 1870—1984 and shows that labor productivity has grown more slowly in the United States than in other countries over the last 40 years, but faster in the preceding 70 years. In addition, the U.S. growth rate has declined since the 1973 oil shocks from its previous levels, which has been a cause of concern about the health of the U.S. economy. However, the long-run data also suggest that all industrial countries experienced a productivity

Table 2.1

Gross Domestic Product per Capita: Indices Using Current PPPs
(OECD=100)

Year	United States	Germany	Japan	France	United Kingdom	EC	OECD
1971	140	105	81	101	92	89	100
1991	125	110	108	103	88	92	100

SOURCE: OECD (1993).

Table 2.2

Growth in Labor Productivity (GDP per Hour Worked)

Country	Period I 1870–1913	Period II 1913–1950	Period III 1950–1973	Period IV 1973–1984	Change from Period II–III	Change from Period III–IV
United States	2.0	2.4	2.5	1.0	+0.1	−1.5
Japan	1.8	1.7	7.7	3.2	+6.0	−4.5
France	1.7	2.0	5.1	3.4	+3.1	−1.7
Germany	1.9	1.0	6.0	3.0	+5.0	−3.0
United Kingdom	1.2	1.6	3.2	2.4	+1.6	−0.8

SOURCE: Maddison (1987); rates are annual average compound growth rates.

slowdown in the 1970s and that this general slowdown is a return to normal growth rates at the end of an unusually fast growth period.[1]

Although labor productivity is a good indicator of economic welfare, changes in labor productivity do not directly measure labor's contribution to economic growth. Labor productivity may change because higher levels of education increase the quality of labor input or because of demographic changes in the composition of the labor force. But labor productivity also improves because of increases in capital equipment per worker and technical progress—even if the level of skills and performance standards do not change simultaneously. The fast growth of labor productivity in postwar Japan is partly due to a higher rate of capital investment than in other OECD countries.

A measure that takes into account the contribution of both labor and capital is total factor productivity (TFP), which measures the output produced for a given amount of labor and capital. TFP is a measure of an economy's efficiency and a high TFP growth rate indicates fast growing returns to both capital and labor. When there are a number of different inputs and outputs whose composition and quality changes over time, productivity growth calculations become a complicated task and there are a number of different but equally legiti-

---

[1]See also Darby (1984), Helliwell, Sturm, and Salou (1985), Baumol, Blackman, and Wolff (1989).

mate ways to calculate TFP growth.[2] One such series of TFP growth rates for 1913–1984 is reported in Table 2.3. Chapter Three provides more details on the calculations and the contribution of education in the last period.

"Competitiveness" at the firm (or even industry) level is an intuitive concept: A competitive firm can produce cheaper than other firms. But it is much less clear what "competitiveness" means when applied to a country as a whole. The long-lasting trade deficit has often been considered to be an indicator that the U.S. economy is not "competitive." This is related to the commonly held view that slower productivity growth compared to other countries invariably causes job losses and deteriorating living standards. According to this belief, firms in the laggard country are at an increasing disadvantage and cannot "compete" against foreign products in the international market. But this ignores an important difference between a firm and a country: A low demand for a country's products (and therefore its currency) causes the exchange rate to fall until the balance of payments is ultimately in equilibrium, regardless of a country's productivity record. International markets depend on comparative, rather than absolute, advantages, and this implies that there are always some sectors in every economy that are internationally competitive after exchange rates adjust. Competitiveness as used in popular

Table 2.3

Total Factor Productivity Growth, 1913–1984

Country	1913–1950	1950–1973	1973–1984
United States	1.19	1.05	−.27
Japan	0.04	4.69	0.43
France	0.61	3.11	0.93
Germany	0.19	3.61	1.13
United Kingdom	0.38	1.53	0.64

SOURCE: Maddison (1987); rates are annual average compound growth rates.

---

[2]A detailed discussion of different productivity concepts and measurement can be found in Baumol and Wolff (1989); Baumol, Blackman, and Wolff (1989, Ch. 11) provide a very accessible introduction.

policy debates should probably be interpreted either as absolute advantages in all or most industries or as comparative advantages in some desirable industries, such as "high technology."

DE-INDUSTRIALIZATION AND CONVERGENCE

It is widely believed that the U.S. economy is losing its industrial core compared to other advanced countries like Japan and Germany. Lawrence (1984), Baumol, Blackman, and Wolff (1989), and Dollar and Wolff (1993) have investigated this de-industrialization thesis for the United States but found little evidence for it.[3] In fact, the United States has slightly increased its share of manufacturing output compared to most other advanced countries: Japan increased its share of manufacturing output in 14 OECD countries from 14 percent in 1970 to 23 percent in 1987 and the United States increased its share from 37 percent to 38 percent, whereas Germany fell from 14 percent to 11 percent and the other OECD countries from 36 percent to 29 percent between 1970 to 1987 (Dollar and Wolff, 1993, pp. 24–25). The picture for exports is somewhat different; there the United States has experienced a general decline in its share of world trade. Dollar and Wolff show that the United States did better in technology-intensive and high-technology industries[4] than in other manufacturing industries. Chemicals and most equipment and machinery industries, including automobiles, experienced the heaviest losses. Thus, actual data do not support the belief that the U.S. comparative advantages are shifting away from high-wage industrial products to low-wage sectors. Unfortunately, the past is not an indicator for the future because comparative advantages not based on climate or natural resources are not permanently fixed and industrial and educational policies may create comparative advantages in certain sectors. This is the main reason for calls by the Clinton Administration and its advisors for a more activist trade policy (Tyson, 1992).

---

[3]Other related research with similar conclusions include Darby (1984), Helliwell, Sturm, and Salou (1985), and Maddison (1987).

[4]Technology-intensive products were defined as products of industries with R&D spending of 5 percent or more of value added or scientific and technical employment of more than 5 percent; high-technology industries have 10 percent or more R&D spending or scientific/technical employment.

Although there is little evidence of de-industrialization or that the United States has experienced decreasing levels of labor productivity, there can be no doubt that other industrial countries have caught up. If the trade-as-war metaphor, where the gain of one party is the loss of another, were correct this should be a cause of concern. But economists tend to view trade as a mutually beneficial exchange and American consumers certainly gain from the fact that Japan can produce higher-quality export goods cheaper than it could twenty years ago. The trade-as-war metaphor is concerned with the relative position of the United States and the potential loss of the world's economic leadership. Economic leadership may contribute to national pride, political power, or military strength, but it is an indicator of only relative, not absolute, economic welfare. Since the United Kingdom lost its position as the world's economic leader around 1879, output per work hour has increased by a factor of six and exports by a factor of nine in the United Kingdom (Maddison, 1987; Baumol, Blackman, Wolff, 1989).

Economists have long argued that per capita GDP or labor productivity levels converge across countries (Gerschenkron, 1962): Countries learn about new productive techniques through trade, technology transfer, and their own R&D efforts. Although all countries benefit from technology transfer, the follower countries have more to learn from the technology leaders than the technology leaders can learn from other countries.[5] But this catchup mechanism is only temporary: As the gap between countries narrows, the relative benefits of learning change in favor of the leaders. U.S. firms had very little to learn from Japanese firms in the 1950s but adopted many Japanese process technologies and management approaches in the 1980s. Figure 2.1 shows the convergence trend for 1950 to 1988. Earlier research has shown that the convergence among industrialized countries started more than 100 years ago (Maddison, 1987).

There are factors affecting economic growth in addition to the convergence driven by technology transfer. An essential factor is a country's "social capability" (Abramowitz, 1986), i.e., the ability to exploit the "advantages of backwardness" by copying the production

---

[5]However, even the leader's productivity would grow slower without technology transfer from follower countries. Spillover effects have been estimated many times, most recently by Mohnen (1992); see also the review by Reddy and Zhao (1990).

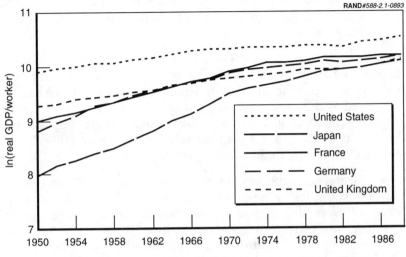

SOURCE: Penn World Table (Mark 5), data set described in Summers and Heston (1991).

Figure 2.1—Convergence Trends in Labor Productivity

methods of the leader without incurring the same development costs. The level of education (and, in less developed countries, the level of literacy) are important elements of a country's social capability. Even though there has been a dramatic convergence of labor productivity among the OECD countries, African and many Asian countries are excluded from this "convergence club." However, the general trend for convergence reappears after controlling for several key variables measuring social capability: education, investment, and trade orientation. Low levels of education and investment or inward orientation (compared to unrestricted trade and an open economy) slow down growth and may prevent countries from catching up with the leaders. Baumol, Blackman, and Wolff (1989) find different convergence groups by education levels, i.e., countries with comparable levels of education are converging among themselves, but they do not close the gap to countries with higher educational levels. Most important appears to be the level of secondary education; primary education alone (universal literacy) may not be sufficient for adopting and implementing new technology. However, there does not appear to be a need for a large college-educated workforce.

Barro's analysis (1991) yields similar results: The direct correlation between GDP per capita growth and initial level of GDP per capita is close to zero, but the correlation becomes substantially negative as predicted by the convergence hypothesis after controlling for initial levels of school-enrollment rates. Poorer countries catch up with the leaders as long as they have relatively high levels of schooling in comparison to their initial level of GDP per capita.

The convergence hypothesis falls short of explaining changes in the ranks of countries in their relative productivity and there certainly have been several such changes over the last centuries. Even though the data show convergence and not that the United States is quickly surpassed by other countries, it is important to consider factors that may allow countries to "forge ahead" or to "fall behind" (Abramowitz, 1986). Nelson and Wright (1992) see two conceptually distinct components in the postwar American technological lead: a strength in mass production industries and a lead in high-technology industries. Market opportunities were essential for the advantage in mass production industries and European countries, which may have had the social capabilities, were limited by small internal markets and trade barriers to follow U.S. development. Nelson and Wright argue that, in contrast to mass production, European countries and Japan may have lacked the social capabilities to succeed in high-technology industries until they followed the United States in making similar investments in scientific and engineering education and R&D.

But these two distinct sources of leadership may erode. The globalization of trade allows other countries to serve large markets. Moreover, institutions age and an economic structure that was successful during one period of economic development may be less successful in another period, causing a country to fall behind (Dertouzos et al., 1989; Lazonick, 1990; Reich, 1991). In a world where the production strategy for high-value goods moves away from mass production, it may not be an advantage to have been the leader in mass production techniques. Regarding the other source of leadership, the spillover effects from military R&D appear to be reduced, partly because the military demands have shifted away from areas that have civilian as well as military applications (Nelson, 1990), indicating that the old structure of R&D funding has become obsolete. These important additional considerations qualify the findings of economic data analyses.

Nevertheless, it is important to keep in mind that some commonly held beliefs about the U.S. economic performance are not supported by actual data. Careful economic analyses find no evidence of de-industrialization or shifts toward "low-technology" export industries. Japan or other countries are not quickly surpassing the United States on their way to dominating the U.S. economy but are slowly catching up as part of a general convergence process among industrialized countries. Current findings may not be reassuring about the *relative* U.S. position and do not provide guarantees for the future. However, it is also true that "the longer-run data constitute no grounds for hysteria or recourse to ill-considered measures that are grasped at in a mood of desperation" (Baumol, Blackman, and Wolff, 1989, p. 6).

Chapter Three

THE CONTRIBUTION OF EDUCATION TO ECONOMIC GROWTH

The fast growth of real income or GDP per capita over the last century cannot be explained by capital accumulation or more labor input alone (Solow, 1957; Kendrick, 1961; Denison, 1962) and economists have tried to measure the sources of economic growth by analyzing changes in the quality of labor and capital, changes in the economic and policy environment, and technical progress. The so-called growth accounting approach has provided some of the most cited estimates of the contribution of education to economic growth. However, even researchers citing these estimates are not always aware of the limitations of growth accounting. Some potential misunderstandings are clarified in this section.

THE GROWTH ACCOUNTING APPROACH

Education's contribution is traditionally estimated by some variant of an accounting framework which assumes that there exists an aggregate production function for the economy. This production function links output to various inputs such as labor and physical capital. Growth accounting divides the credit for output growth into the contributions of changes in various inputs. Changes in input *quantities* alone leave a large unexplained residual, and most research therefore adds changes in input *quality*, such as a more productive labor force through higher levels of education.[1]

---

[1]Studies considering the effect of education on labor quality include Baumol and McLennan (1985); Baumol, Blackman, and Wolff (1989); Denison (1962, 1967, 1974, 1979, 1980, 1983); Jorgenson, Gollop, and Fraumeni (1987); Jorgenson and Fraumeni

Although growth accounting provides a useful and widely accepted framework to organize relevant facts, compare countries, and identify areas that need a deeper investigation, its focus is quite narrow. The residual (the part of economic growth that is not explained by the model) is often taken as a measure of "technological change" or TFP growth and the estimates of education's contribution to economic growth capture only the "direct" effect of education, i.e., they answer the hypothetical question of how changes in the quality of labor would affect output if everything else stayed constant. They do not address any of the interaction between different causes of growth, such as the links between education and technical progress, education and capital growth, or technical progress and capital growth. But such complementarities are likely to be important. Dollar and Wolff (1993) and Wolff (1991) emphasize positive complementarities between capital investment and technological progress, especially for laggard countries catching up with leaders. In particular, the demand for investment depends on the opportunity for the introduction of new technology: Recent technological progress in computers has stimulated large investments in information technology. Technological change is not exogenous either, but depends on knowledge creation and diffusion with its close links to the education sector. Finally, economists have found complementarities between high-skill labor and capital accumulation (Griliches, 1969). Consequently, the growth accounting estimates of technological change or (total factor) productivity growth are often misunderstood: If education or other quality improvements are included in a growth accounting analysis, they reduce, rather than increase, TFP growth, because they explain some of the residual.

Growth accounting estimates of the contribution of education have been criticized for other reasons. Plant and Welch (1984) demonstrate that the standard techniques may be inappropriate for education and other forms of intermediate inputs into the production process, although their theoretical alternative to measure the contribution of education to economic growth has not received much attention. Measurement is another difficult issue: (1) education is largely estimated by the amount of formal education in the pop-

---

(1991); Kendrick (1973, 1977, 1984); Maddison (1974, 1982, 1984, 1987); and Weisskopf, Bowles, and Gordon (1983).

ulation and there are no adjustments for the quality of education; (2) there are few data on changes in education and training services other than formal education, i.e., training in firms; and (3) calculations are based on information recorded in the national income accounts, which excludes all nonmarket transactions.[2]

ESTIMATING THE ROLE OF EDUCATION IN ECONOMIC GROWTH

Despite its limitations, growth accounting can show how the contribution of education to economic growth can be calculated and how such estimates compare across countries. Maddison (1982, 1987) provides detailed data for several industrialized countries and a transparent discussion of the necessary building blocks, which is used here. As Table 2.2 showed, the period from 1973 to 1984 is of particular interest because labor productivity growth in the United States declined from its previous levels and much of the policy discussion concerned about the U.S. performance remains influenced by analyses performed on data from this period.

The first column in Table 3.1 repeats the measure of labor productivity growth of Table 2.2. The second column reports a very crude measure of total factor productivity growth: the growth rate of real GDP minus the weighted average of the rates of capital and labor increase, with weights related to the factor shares in GDP (residential and nonresidential capital is distinguished). But the crude estimate of TFP growth is unsatisfactory because it ignores quality changes in the inputs, for example, better educated workers. Thus, a part of the "exogenous" technical progress (TFP growth) may really be due to increases in education levels. Column 3 reports TFP growth after adjusting for the quality of labor and capital input and reveals that the economic growth in the United States has only been due to changes in the quality of inputs during this period: Had the quality stayed constant, GDP would have declined. Column 4 corrects for additional factors such as changes in the economic structure, government regulation, trade effects, and crime. Thus the negative

---

[2]See Griliches (1969), Kendrick (1977), Nelson (1981), Psacharopoulos (1984), and Maddison (1987) for a discussion of measurement problems and other criticisms of growth accounting estimates.

Table 3.1

Productivity and the Contribution of Labor Quality Changes to Economic Growth, 1973–1984

	Labor Produc- tivity Growth	Crude TFP Growth	TFP Growth Adjusted for Labor and Capital Quality Only	TFP Growth Including Supplementary Factors	Education Growth	Contribution of Labor Quality to Growth (% points)
France	3.4	1.84	0.93	0.59	0.85	0.48
Germany	3.0	1.55	1.13	0.69	0.14	0.07
Japan	3.2	1.21	0.43	0.04	0.63	0.41
United Kingdom	2.4	1.22	0.64	0.49	0.45	0.20
United States	1.0	0.52	−0.27	−0.01	0.77	0.36

SOURCE: Maddison (1987); numbers are annual average compound growth rates, except for the last column, which are percentage points.

residual that was found for the United States after adjusting for quality changes in input was not technical regress or "forgetting," but was caused by other structural effects. The main negative factors were crime, regulation, and energy with a combined annual damaging effect of 0.28 percentage points.

To calculate the contribution of education, it is necessary to derive an index of how education affects the quality of the labor force. This entails some ad hoc assumptions: How does a year of secondary education differ from a year of primary education or a year of college education? This, of course, is not independent from the economic situation. As Baumol, Blackman, and Wolff (1989) found in their test of the convergence hypotheses, the levels of secondary education were more important than the levels of primary education in determining a less-developed country's convergence class. Weighting a year of primary education by 1, a year of secondary education by 1.4, and a year of higher education by 2.0 gives rise to the growth rate of average population education in the column "education growth."[3]

----

[3]There is no theoretical basis for calculating the weights—they are an ad hoc assumption. As before, we have to distinguish levels and growth rates; the level of

The quality of secondary or higher education is likely to differ even among advanced industrialized countries and perhaps even the weights should differ. No adjustment has been made for changes in nonformal education.

This education index for the population is then weighted with other sociodemographic changes in the labor force to calculate the contribution of labor quality. Here, only changes in the sex mix of the labor force are included, but more detailed measures are possible. Jorgenson and Fraumeni (1991), for example, distinguish over 2000 different types of labor input by age, sex, experience, education, etc. The overall effect of education on economic growth is typically reported as in the final column "contribution of labor quality to growth."

According to these estimates, Germany had the lowest and France and Japan the highest contribution of education to economic growth. The United States takes a position in the middle among the group of industrialized countries. Thus, the lower growth rates in the United States compared to other countries cannot be ascribed to smaller increases in labor quality. Of course, these estimates are subject to the criticisms mentioned before. If Germany invested heavily in nonformal education and less in formal education, the estimated contribution of education is low and the contribution of training would be captured in TFP growth. Column 4 shows that Germany had the highest TFP growth corrected for input quality changes and supplementary factors (but excluding unmeasured effects such as training). This would be consistent with the hypothesis that formal educational achievement is less important than the availability and growth of skilled labor. Haskel and Martin (1993) consider the effect of skill shortages on U.K. productivity and conclude that productivity growth was reduced by 0.7 percent annually during the 1980s because of increasing skill shortages. School quality is another unmeasured effect that might bias growth accounting estimates. If schools are worse in the United States than in other coun-

---

education in the United States was higher than in the other countries. In terms of average years of formal education in the population aged 15–64 years in 1984, the numbers are 10.79 in France, 9.48 in Germany, 11.15 in Japan, 9.92 in the Netherlands, 10.92 in the United Kingdom, and 12.52 in the United States. The weighted indices are 13.65 (France), 11.86 (Germany), 13.56 (Japan), 11.83 (Netherlands), 13.14 (United Kingdom), and 16.18 (United States).

tries, the growth accounting framework might overstate the contribution of education in the United States. Bishop (1989) considered the changes in the quality of education measured by test scores and reported a substantial negative effect of the test score decline on labor quality and GNP.[4] Unfortunately, it appears that no other studies have adjusted for these possible effects using explicit measured training or school quality.[5]

Regardless of the particular calculation, education and its effect through labor quality are generally found to be among the most important contributors to economic growth. The studies by Denison and Kendrick in Dean (1984) find that education contributed 15–25 percent of growth in per capita GDP. Jorgenson (in Dean, 1984) estimates that education is responsible for 38 percent of the contribution of labor, accounting for over 90 percent in the change in labor quality. Even economists who cannot be suspected of favoring any form of social policy acknowledge the importance of education and call for a higher priority on educational policy:

> Given the importance of investment in education for long term economic growth, economists and policy makers have devoted far too little attention to the implications of educational policy. The magnitude of investment in education dwarfs that of conventional forms of investment, such as investment in tangible assets. The most important component of the educational investment is the value of the time that individuals choose to devote to formal education. Investments by individuals are largely motivated by higher lifetime labor incomes associated with higher educational attainment. Educational policy can affect individual decisions by financing participation in the education system and expanding the capacity of educational institutions. (Jorgenson and Fraumeni, 1991, p. 3).

Jorgenson and Fraumeni (1991) present the most recent major research on the link between education and growth for the United

---

[4]He estimates that labor quality would have been 2.9 percent higher and GNP $86 billion higher in 1987 if test scores had grown at the same rate after 1967 as they did in the preceding quarter century.

[5]Haskel and Martin measure skill shortages by the percentage of firms within an industry reporting output constraints because of a shortage of skilled labor.

States and their main contribution is to extend the output measure of the education sector by including the value of time spent outside the labor market. They justify this step because of the nonmarket benefits that education provides, i.e., education is not only a producer good that enhances an individual's productivity but also a consumer good that yields direct benefits. Thus, excluding the increase in the value of leisure would underestimate the benefits of education. At least for the noneducation sector, their findings are quite comparable to earlier research. For 1973–1979, they estimate the contribution of labor quality to be 0.15 percentage points and from 1979–1986 0.35 percentage points in the noneducation sector.

Psacharopoulos (1984) compiled a different set of estimates for a diverse set of countries (see Table 3.2). He does not provide details about the calculations or data, but they appear to be for the years until the early 1970s. Because the numbers may be calculated very differently, a direct comparison of the numbers for the earlier years reported by Psacharopoulos with the period 1973–1984 is questionable. However, it appears reasonable that education explains a larger fraction in the later years because of the slowdown of TFP growth (technological progress). A surprising feature is the large variance of the role of education in economic growth across countries. To my knowledge, there has been no investigation of this phenomenon. Some of this variation might be caused by differences in the composition of outputs. Service sectors, for example, are measured as having slow rates of productivity growth (although researchers, e.g., Bailey and Gordon, 1988, have argued that this may be measurement error). Thus, the same growth in educational achievement would have a smaller estimated absolute effect on growth in a more service-oriented economy but might explain more of its growth because of the larger role of human resources. Incomplete measures of ET and differences across countries along unmeasured dimensions of ET is another likely explanation.

Table 3.2

Percentage of Growth "Explained" by Education

Country	Growth Rate Explained (until 1970s)[a]	Growth Rate Explained (1973–1984)[b]
North America		
Canada	25.0	n.a.
United States	15.0	15.5
Europe		
Belgium	14.0	n.a.
Denmark	4.0	n.a.
France	6.0	22.0
Germany	2.0	4.2
Italy	7.0	n.a.
Greece	3.0	n.a.
Netherlands	5.0	20.9
Norway	7.0	n.a.
United Kingdom	12.0	18.9
USSR	6.7	n.a.
Latin America		
Argentina	16.5	n.a.
Brazil	3.3	n.a.
Chile	4.5	n.a.
Colombia	4.1	n.a.
Equador	4.9	n.a.
Honduras	6.5	n.a.
Peru	2.5	n.a.
Mexico	0.8	n.a.
Venezuela	2.4	n.a.
Asia		
Japan	3.3	10.8
Malaysia	14.7	n.a.
Philippines	10.5	n.a.
South Korea	15.9	n.a.
Africa		
Ghana	23.2	n.a.
Kenya	12.4	n.a.
Nigeria	16.0	n.a.

[a]Psacharopoulos (1984, p. 337).
[b]My calculations based on Maddison's data (1987).

Chapter Four

THE ECONOMIC RETURNS TO EDUCATION AND TRAINING

The positive correlation between ET and wages/income has stimulated many attempts to establish a causal connection at the microeconomic level. Originally motivated by the puzzles of macroeconomic growth (Schultz, 1961), the human capital theory developed by Schultz (1961, 1963), Becker (1962, 1964, 1975), and Mincer (1962, 1974) dominates the literature. The theory of human capital considers education as an investment that makes individuals more productive and focuses on pecuniary gains. To invest in additional schooling and training, which is never free because it requires at least time taken away from other opportunities, an individual must expect higher lifetime earnings according to this theory. But in a competitive economy, an individual has to be more productive to receive a higher income.[1]

If ET enables individuals to produce more efficiently, it can lower the costs to produce additional output and can shift the supply curve. Figure 4.1 demonstrates the effect in a simple static model.[2] The new producer surplus is the area ACBA (the producers would have supplied the first units for less money than they actually received); the new consumer surplus is the area BCDB (the consumers would have paid more for the first units than they did); the total surplus is the sum of the two areas (ACDA). This is a social gain from the previ-

---

[1] Blaug (1976, 1985) has critically reviewed the human capital foundation of the economics of education.

[2] It may be easiest to assume that the shift in the supply curve is caused by an exogenous shock in the ET environment. The introduction of primary schooling in rural areas in some developing countries would be an example.

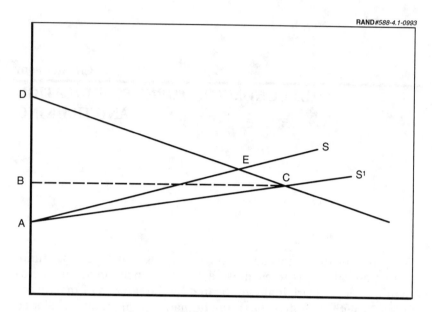

Figure 4.1—Macroeconomic Effects

ous state as long as the difference between the old and the new total surplus (the area ACEA) is larger than the costs of ET that shifted the supply from S to S'. Figure 4.1 provides one example in which data on earnings alone permit only limited calculation of social returns to education.

Welch (1970) calls this productive value of education the "worker effect" and defines it as the increased output per unit change in education holding other inputs constant (the shift in the supply curve in Figure 4.1 already takes into account changes in other inputs in response to the (exogenous) increase in education).

A complementary explanation of the human capital effect suggests that ET improves allocative skills (Nelson and Phelps, 1966; Welch, 1970; Schultz, 1975, 1984): In a changing or growing economy, individuals with higher levels of schooling can better evaluate new opportunities because they distinguish more easily between the random and systematic components of economic change. Better-educated individuals can take advantage of new production and service possibilities or adjust existing techniques to new market situations more quickly than less-educated individuals. Bartel and Lichtenberg (1987) provide evidence for the hypothesis that highly educated workers have a comparative advantage in implementing new technology. This (dynamic) allocative effect of education can exist in addition to the (static) worker effect. Individuals who exploit new opportunities gain relative to individuals who are slower to respond, but competition quickly translates these efficiency gains into lower prices or better products and services. The sooner new opportunities are exploited and efficient production methods adopted, the larger the gain for consumers and social benefits.[3] The same, of course, is true for services.

Although coming out of the human capital tradition, the dynamic disequilibrium models of the allocative effect by Welch (1970) and Schultz (1975) incorporate the role of "entrepreneurial capacity" into the competitive model. They have different implications for the social benefits of education than the static equilibrium models that dominate the returns-to-education literature (see the next section on the wage/earnings equation). In particular, the returns to education (under the allocative skills interpretation) rise if the rate of technical change increases or the gap between available technology and technology in use widens. Similarly, the incentives for acquiring education are based on the dynamics of economic change: In a stagnant economy, the returns to superior allocative skills are small, lowering the overall levels of education. This allocative role may be one of the most important issues for the current policy discussion. Unfortunately, this branch of microeconomic studies of education is very small.

The major competing framework to the human capital approach is the screening hypothesis, suggested by Arrow (1973), Spence (1973), and others. According to the screening hypothesis (in its extreme form), education does not improve an individual's productivity. Instead, education is seen as a sorting mechanism that distinguishes inherently more-productive from less-productive individuals and assigns them to occupations. Higher expected wages provide the in-

---

[3]This is not to deny that there will be losers among the people slower to respond, but the social gains are such that income could be redistributed to make everybody better off.

centive to invest in the signal of being a more productive individual, i.e., to become educated. As in the human capital model, higher wages for more-educated workers are only feasible if these workers are more productive, requiring that the sorting mechanism effectively distinguish more- from less-productive individuals.[4]

The screening and human capital theories are similar as far as the correlations between income, productivity, and education are concerned. Consequently, there are no convincing tests that would distinguish the two theories using observational data (Riley, 1979; Willis, 1986). Willis (1986) demonstrates with an example that the same observable data are consistent with both theories, even though one could easily determine the causation between education and productivity with experimental data. Many empirical studies have therefore claimed erroneously that education increases an individual's productivity; in fact, they could not distinguish the sorting from the productivity-enhancing role of education (see, for example, Lazear's comment (1977) on Wise (1975)).

Under the screening hypothesis, the social rate of return is the rate of return to sorting individuals into different occupations; under the human capital view, it is the return to the investment in improving the quality of the labor force. Even though screening does not improve the quality of the labor force, it can increase the efficiency of an economy by assigning people to jobs that correspond to their comparative advantages. The social returns to education under the screening hypothesis have not been estimated, but such estimates might lead to different conclusions than the human capital theory. Of course, the strong version of the screening hypothesis is untenable, but there will be some element of screening in every ET system.

The idea of credentialism in the noneconomic literature, the "diploma disease" (Dore, 1976) or "paper qualifications syndrome" (International Labor Organization, 1981, 1982), is related to the screening hypothesis. It suggests that expanding the educational system is unlikely to improve economic welfare because hiring standards will simply be upgraded. Dore and Oxenham (1984) perceive

---

[4]Sorting according to productivity is the simplest interpretation. The primary achievement of the education sector suggested in this literature is to detect comparative advantages and to sort individuals into the appropriate occupations.

the move toward making education a pure sorting mechanism, which could (although the authors qualify that statement immediately) "lead to a universal, identical and irretrievable downward spiral to complete educational disaster" (p. 29). Although the discussions generally provide much more institutional detail than economic studies, they are only partial analyses; they focus on the education sector but ignore its interaction with the economy as a whole.

Both the human capital and the screening theory maintain the assumption that earnings reflect productivity, but every economist would concede that the relationship between wages and productivity can break down. This is particularly likely in sectors that are not subject to the pressure of market forces, such as government or state-run companies. In addition, there is the problem of measuring an individual's contribution to a firm's productivity. The relationship between education and earnings may become institutionalized and the possession of a qualification may entitle a worker to higher pay regardless of performance. If the government sector is large, this can lead to substantial distortions in the private sector labor market. Little (1984) discusses how wages are determined for government employees in Sri Lanka and Kenya and demonstrates that institutionalized wage setting drives a wedge between wages and productivity and explains the "diploma disease" in this sector. The Jobs and Skills Program for Africa run by the International Labor Organization (1981, 1982) reports a similar finding. Unionization may exert a similar effect in the private sector.

Other theories can explain part of the observed correlation between education and income, although they are less encompassing than either the human capital or the screening theory (Blaug, 1976, 1985): job competition, labor market segmentation, nonclearing wages, social class, and institutionalized wages in the public sector. For firm-specific wage growth, two more recent types of arguments are often found in the economics literature. Job matching models, introduced by Jovanovic (1979), suggest that imperfect information about job and worker characteristics may be one reason for observed wages to be higher with longer tenure. Poor matches, i.e., workers being unproductive in a certain job, are likely to be broken soon as workers search for more appropriate jobs or employers for better suited workers, whereas good matches are likely to last longer. But there is no guarantee that wages reflect current productivity: Becker and

Stigler (1974), Lazear (1979), Harris and Holmstrom (1982), and others have demonstrated that it can be efficient for a firm to separate wages from current productivity to discourage workers from shirking.[5]

THE HUMAN CAPITAL EARNINGS/WAGE FUNCTION

The primary tool used to investigate the relationship between ET and productivity at the individual level has been the earnings or wage function, which received a consistent human capital foundation by Mincer (1974), but which dates back as an empirical tool to the 1940s and 1950s (Griliches, 1977). The earnings function postulates that there exists a relationship between ET (S), experience and other factors (X), and earnings (Y):

$$\ln Y_i = \alpha + \beta S_i + X_i \gamma + u_i$$

Human capital theory can justify this particular functional form analytically, but many researchers have taken a more statistical approach by letting the data determine the functional form.

The human capital earnings function is considered to be one of the major success stories in empirical economics, although institutionalized wages are a case where investigating the positive relationship between education and earnings may not provide the deep insights about the workings of an economy that economists are hoping for. Literally thousands of studies have estimated the earnings equation or the returns to education and there exists a large and sophisticated literature on the statistical problems of estimating this equation and its interpretation (Griliches, 1977; Willis, 1986). The theoretical human capital justification of the wage equation is based on the assumption that markets clear and are in equilibrium. The dynamic elements of the models consider how an individual's human capital changes over time; the environment is generally taken as stationary. Thus, the concept of the wage equation differs fundamentally from

---

[5]These papers belong to the recent research stream of *principal-agent* models, which differs from the neoclassical human capital framework in the central role of imperfect information in economic interactions.

the ideas behind the disequilibrium models of Welch (1970) and Schultz (1975) or the macroeconomic growth literature.

From an economic point of view, an analysis of earnings and education should consider the supply of human capital, the demand for it, and the market equilibrium simultaneously. Freeman (1971) has provided evidence of the equilibrating mechanism of the labor market, analyzing the demand and supply of human capital in specialized fields of study, but other authors have not found his analysis convincing (Blaug, 1976). However, by far the largest group of studies considers only the supply side of the human capital theory by studying the returns to education using the wage equation. Nevertheless, the wage equation by itself can provide important insights about the productive mechanism in the economy under certain assumptions: If there exist different types of labor, which differ in their productivity but which can otherwise substitute for each other, a competitive market will establish wages that reflect the marginal productivity of each type of labor. The wage equation is typically interpreted as a hedonic equation for labor, which reflects the market equilibrium between supply and demand for each amount of human capital (educated worker). This interpretation is not without its problems, of course (Rosen, 1974; Willis, 1986). For example, the estimated parameters for education correspond to the current market opportunities, but not necessarily to the expectations of individuals when they decided to invest in education.

SOCIAL AND PRIVATE RETURNS TO EDUCATION

Statistical earnings functions have been estimated since the 1960s to measure the internal rate of return to education (Becker, 1964; Hanoch, 1967). The internal rate of return is the discount rate r that equalizes the present values of the lifetime earnings associated with different levels of education, i.e., it solves the equation

$$\sum_{t=0}^{T} \frac{Y_{st} - Y_{s-1,t} - C_{st}}{(1+r)^t} = 0$$

where Y_{st} are the (adjusted) net earnings of workers with an education level of s in period t, $Y_{s-1,t}$ are the earnings of workers with the next lower level of schooling, and C_{st} are the costs of obtaining the education level s in year t.

The private returns to education and training can be estimated relatively easily from earnings data. The studies by Becker (1964), Hanoch (1967), and Mincer (1974) showed a pattern of decreasing marginal private rates of return to schooling, suggesting that it may be efficient to redistribute educational expenses. But the pattern of decreasing returns may be caused by imperfectly measured incomes or costs: Low estimates of the returns to graduate studies can reflect unmeasured fellowships that lower an individual's costs of education; jobs requiring higher levels of education may provide additional side benefits not captured by wages. All of these studies assume that higher wages reflect higher productivity.

It has been argued that the rates of return to college started to fall in the 1970s (Freeman, 1976; Psacharopoulos, 1981), but there is some evidence that the rate of return stayed between 8 and 9 percent until the early 1980s and has since risen (Willis, 1986); see Table 4.1. The rates-of-return literature may also shed some light on the deskilling discussion in the sociology literature (Braverman, 1974; Attewell, 1987), which essentially is a demand side argument. The deskilling hypothesis claims that technological change leads to the reorganization of jobs, producing lower skill levels for the majority of workers.[6] Lowering required skill levels (except for a small elite) should increase the demand for less-skilled workers and lower the demand for higher-skilled workers, thus reducing the rates of return to education without a corresponding change in supply. This is not consistent with the developments of the last decade: Bound and Johnson (1992) compare several alternative explanations for relative wage changes and conclude that the major cause of the increased skill premium was a shift in the skill structure of labor demand brought about by biased technological change. Murphy and Welch (1992) report that college graduates earned 29 percent more per hour than high school graduates in 1980 and that this differential increased to 69 percent by the end of the decade. Katz and Murphy (1992) find a general trend

---

[6]There exists a related economic literature on the employment distribution effects of capital investment (Griliches, 1969; Berndt, Morrison, and Rosenblum, 1992; Freeman, Clark, and Soete, 1982), but generally with opposite conclusions; see also Capelli (1991b).

Table 4.1

Private Returns to Education in the United States
(internal rate in %)

Year	(a) Secondary Education	(b) Higher Education	(c) Higher Education
1959	10.1	11.3	n.a.
1969	10.7	10.9	9.0
1974	14.8	4.8	8.5
1979	n.a.	n.a.	7.9
1982	n.a.	n.a.	10.2

SOURCE: Willis (1986, p. 537), based on Psacharopoulos (1981) (columns a and b) and unpublished calculations by Welch (column c).

n.a. = not available.

toward increased skill premiums and the 1970s decline appears to have been an exception (Table 4.2).

The private returns to education are less important for educational planning than the social returns. Social returns should include estimates of social benefits and costs that accrue to other persons than the individual educated. Such externalities play a central role in the efficient sharing of educational costs between society and individuals. Recent economic studies of the allocation of human resources (Baumol, 1990; Murphy, Shleifer, and Vishny, 1991) focus on the gap

Table 4.2

U.S. Real Weekly Wage Changes for Full-Time Employed Men, 1963–1987

Experience and Years of Education	1963–1971	1971–1979	1979–1987	1963–1987
1–5 years experience; education				
< 12	20.5	1.5	−15.8	6.2
12	17.4	0.8	−19.8	−1.6
16+	18.9	−11.3	10.8	18.4
26–35 years experience; education				
<12	19.3	−0.4	−1.9	17.0
12	14.3	3.2	−2.8	14.7
16+	28.1	−4.0	1.8	25.9

SOURCE: Katz and Murphy (1992), change in log average real weekly wage * 100.

between private and social returns, which varies across occupations. If the private returns to "rent seeking" occupations (i.e., occupations that redistribute wealth without creating new wealth, e.g., divorce lawyers) are higher than the private returns to occupations that generate new knowledge or introduce new technology (and therefore have additional social benefits), human capital is improperly allocated. Murphy, Shleifer, and Vishny (1991) have found that economies with a higher proportion of engineering college majors grow faster and economies with a higher proportion of lawyers grow slower.[7] These considerations further qualify growth accounting estimates that consider total human capital but not its allocation. The social benefits of knowledge creation have also become a central feature of recent developments in growth theory (Romer, 1986, 1990; Grossman and Helpman, 1991).

Unfortunately, the existing estimates of social returns to education are less ambitious than necessary to answer these questions and they differ from the private rates only by subtracting the direct costs paid by society and adding taxes. Externalities and the effects on technical change are ignored, rendering this formulation of social rates of return inadequate to evaluate different educational policies. Psacharopoulos (1975, 1980, 1981, 1985) and Psacharopoulos and Woodhall (1985) have reviewed this literature and Table 4.3 summarizes the results for 44 countries by region or country type. The main conclusions from this line of research are:

- Estimated rates of return are negatively related to the economic wealth of a country;

- The U.S. rates of return are similar to those of other advanced countries;

- The most profitable educational investment in most developing countries is in primary education;

- The returns to investment in human capital are higher than those to physical capital investment in developing countries; the

---

[7]They present two sets of estimates, one for 91 countries and one for countries with more than 10,000 college students (55 countries) and control for investment, general literacy (primary school enrollment), government consumption, political stability, and initial per capita GDP.

Table 4.3
International Comparison of the Returns to Education
(internal rate in %)

Region/ Country Type	No. of Countries	Private Returns to Education			Social Returns to Education		
		Primary	Secondary	Higher	Primary	Secondary	Higher
Africa	9	29	22	32	29	17	12
Asia	8	32	17	19	16	12	11
Latin America	5	24	20	23	44	17	18
Intermediate	8	20	17	17	16	14	10
Advanced	14	n.a.	14	12	n.a.	10	9

SOURCE: Psacharopoulos (1981). n.a. = not applicable.

returns to human capital are similar or even lower in developed countries;

- The social returns to higher education (estimated in the very limited way discussed above) in developing countries are so low that expansion of this sector should be limited; primary and secondary schooling should receive absolute priority;

- The substitutability among differently educated workers is high, thus removing the main argument for manpower planning models;

- Emigration is higher among better-educated workers; in particular, there is a strong economic incentive for highly educated persons in developing countries to emigrate to developed countries (brain drain).

In addition to the inadequacy of measuring social returns to education, cross-country comparisons are less useful to evaluate policies than comparable studies within a single country would be. Estimates for each country include the influence of many institutional factors that are difficult to measure and generally ignored, such as the organization of the ET system, economic and regulatory structures, and the political system. An educational planner would like to know how changing a part of the ET system within a country (for example, placing a higher proportion of university graduates in the labor force) affects productivity or returns to education. But the numbers for a country that already has a high proportion of university graduates are not very informative because all other institutional settings differ as well. The problems the Thatcher government experienced with adopting U.S. ET policies provide a good example of this difficulty (Finegold et al., 1993). Thus, the policy implications of rate-of-return estimates are limited.

TRAINING

Training plays an important role in transmitting specialized knowledge necessary for a particular job and the Office of Technology Assessment (1990) has claimed that American workers are less productive than their foreign counterparts because of inadequate training. In a changing economic environment, training may also become an important element in adapting a worker's skill to new requirements. The issue of training has not been ignored in the economics literature: Becker (1962, 1964) introduced the distinction between general and specific human capital[8] and Mincer (1962) provided the first estimates of the returns to training. However, much more effort has since been devoted to studying the effects of formal education. This situation is to a large extent due to the lack of appropriate data and the difficulty of measuring training in a less-formal setting. Most early studies had to approximate specific human capital or training by overall work experience or job tenure because of the lack of explicit measures.[9] The Equal Opportunity Pilot Project (EOPP) is a relatively recent dataset with more detailed measures on training used by Barron, Black, and Loewenstein (1987, 1989), Holzer (1990), and others. Whereas other datasets, like the Panel Study of Income Dynamics, the National Longitudinal Samples, or the Survey of Income and Program Participation, are based on surveys of individuals or households, the EOPP is a survey of employers.

Studies investigating the effect of private-sector training on earnings generally found a strong positive correlation between private-sector

---

[8]General human capital raises the productivity of a worker regardless of the firm, specific human capital raises a worker's productivity only in a specific firm.

[9]Lillard and Tan (1986) departed from the traditional reliance on such proxy variables by using explicit training measures from five different surveys. However, their report confirms that only the more formal kinds of training tend to be reported in these datasets.

training and wage growth (Barron, Black, and Loewenstein, 1987, 1989; Bartel 1989, 1991, 1992; Blanchflower and Lynch, 1992; Brown, 1989; Duncan and Hoffman, 1979; Holzer, 1990; Lillard and Tan, 1986; Lynch, 1989, 1992). However, wage growth may not be a good measure of the effect of training in these observational studies unless one can separate the training effect from the selection bias that arises because workers do not receive training randomly. Lillard and Tan (1986) have studied who receives training and Barron, Black, and Loewenstein (1987, 1989) suggest that the process by which workers with different abilities are matched to jobs requiring various amounts of training is a key feature of on-the-job training. Thus, it is not possible to conclude that training causes wage growth.

The next step, inferring productivity improvements from wage growth, is also questionable. As mentioned above, there are theoretical arguments suggesting that it can be efficient for a firm to separate pay from current productivity and instead link it to tenure or retirement date.[10]   Direct studies of productivity, discussed in the following section, have tried to circumvent this problem.

Not all training is provided in the private sector. The U.S. Congress has initiated a series of training programs to raise the earnings of unemployed and low-income workers, starting with the Manpower Development and Training Act in 1962, followed by the Comprehensive Employment and Training Act (CETA) in 1972, which was replaced by the Job Partnership Training Act in 1982. Ashenfelter and Card (1985) estimated the effectiveness of training for participants in the CETA programs, paying more attention to the statistical problems of nonrandomized data. They concluded that randomized trials are necessary to reliably determine program effects and deplore the almost complete absence of such experimental programs.[11] The data from nonexperimental government programs have been analyzed by many researchers, and early studies include Ashenfelter (1978), Bassi (1983), Bloch (1979), Dickinson, Johnson, and West (1984). Moffitt (1992) provides the most recent review of training programs. There

---

[10]Brown (1989), however, suggests that wage growth within a firm appears to be determined by contemporaneous productivity growth and not by contractual considerations.

[11]Ashenfelter and Card (1985) provide a reference to one randomized trial.

does not appear to be any lack of studies or programs, but the uniqueness of each program and selection problems make reliable and robust estimates impossible.

DIRECT MEASUREMENT OF PRODUCTIVITY

A number of researchers have studied the differences in productivity of more- and less-educated individuals directly. Direct studies of productivity do not require income data and the calculations of social rates of return may be possible if the organization of production is simple, such as in the agricultural sector. The effect of education in agriculture is best studied in a direct productivity approach because of the high prevalence of self-employment, the fragmentation of labor markets (especially in less-developed countries), and because the productivity of individuals is easily related to actual goods that are valued in competitive markets. For complex production organizations, however, studying the productivity of individuals does not provide much insight about the productivity of the organization or the economy unless much more is known about their structural characteristics. There are many more steps between an individual's performance and economic competitiveness, progress, or growth. Economists have therefore preferred to base their analysis on market models using pecuniary data.

Lockheed, Jamison, and Lau (1980) provide a meta-study of the effect of education on farm productivity (see also Jamison and Lau, 1982). The dependent variable in the studies summarized is the output of a field crop or an aggregate of several field crops. Of 37 datasets, a positive relation between education and agricultural productivity was demonstrated in 25 and a negative relation in six, with six datasets excluded for several reasons. Lockheed, Jamison, and Lau conclude that farm productivity increases on the average by 7.4 percent (standard deviation 6.8 percent) if a farmer completes four years of elementary education. The relationship between education and productivity is much stronger in modern or modernizing systems than in traditional ones, indicating a complementarity of technology and education to improve productivity. But it may also reflect an allocative effect of human capital (Welch, 1970; Schultz, 1975) because the modern and modernizing sectors change more quickly. The mean increase in output for four years of education was 1.3 percent under traditional conditions and 9.5 percent under modern or modernizing conditions. Informal education experience through extension or other services also had a positive effect on output. Another review by Psacharopoulos and Woodhall (1985) finds an average rate of return for primary education of about 6 percent and estimates ranging from zero to 25 percent.

Even though the agricultural studies are often cited as important evidence of the positive effects of education on productivity (Psacharopoulos, 1987), they cannot avoid the possibility of confusing cause and effect. Perhaps some farmers were better educated because their parents already owned a farm with better soil, whose higher productivity generated the income to send their children to school. Observational studies alone will not be able to answer this question unambiguously.

Outside the agriculture sector, the evidence has been much more mixed. After studying several U.S. studies, Berg (1970) compared the performance of differently educated workers in a number of occupations, including bank clerks and scientists, and did not find convincing evidence that education improved their individual productivity; Godfrey (1977) compared formal education qualifications and the results of trade tests in Kenya and concluded that schooling did not explain test results. A large number of studies, summarized in Bretz (1989), analyzed the relationship between educational and work performance and the overall lack of a positive relationship is surprising. Little (1984) provides the results for 47 microstudies of the link between level of educational qualifications and individual productivity in private and public modern sector enterprises in Ghana, Mexico, and Sri Lanka. Overall, there is no positive relationship between level of education and productivity for a variety of different types of work at the individual level. Medoff and Abraham (1980) may be one of the best known economic studies challenging the traditional human capital interpretation that experience raises wages because it enhances productivity. Their analysis of the relationship between earnings, productivity, and experience among managerial and professional employees revealed a strong positive correlation between experience and earnings within grade levels, but no or even a negative correlation between experience and performance.

The advantage of the agricultural studies in developing countries is that physical output can be compared for a much broader range of individuals using various production techniques (possibly reflecting varying skill levels). Thus, one can directly study the effect of ET on individual (farm) productivity and easily aggregate to the productivity of a region or country. This is not true in the industrial studies. For example, the studies reported in Little (1984) compared individuals within particular levels of occupation, not across different levels. Put differently, they compare individuals performing the same tasks (and therefore likely to have similar skills). Although this guarantees a comparability of tasks across individuals, the pervasive effect of self-selection also guarantees that a university graduate performing tasks that are typically executed by workers with only secondary education or less is not representative for university graduates: Education and training only helped initially less-able individuals to achieve the same skill level as others to be included in the comparison. Medoff and Abraham's studies (1980, 1981) could be criticized similarly. Studies using a different sampling scheme, for example, comparing recently hired workers in entry-level positions, find positive effects of training on productivity and labor quality (Barron, Black, and Loewenstein, 1987, 1989; Bishop, 1991; Holzer, 1990). Positive effects of higher levels of education on work performance have also been found by Horowitz and Sherman (1980) and Wise (1975).

In general, however, it is not clear how to compare worker productivity at different tasks, a problem that economists typically circumvent by using one performance measure (earnings) and by relying on labor markets to perform the evaluation of an individual's productivity. The direct measurement of agricultural output avoided this intermediate step. Thus, direct studies of the productivity of individual workers have been very revealing for the agricultural sector in developing countries, but they have not furthered our understanding of competitiveness or economic growth in industrialized countries.

Chapter Five

PRODUCTIVITY GROWTH IN BUSINESS ORGANIZATIONS AND THE EVOLUTION OF THE ECONOMY

Technical progress has been one of the main determinants of the tenfold increase of U.S. labor productivity (GDP per work hour) over the last 100 years (Maddison, 1982, 1987). The theoretical framework underlying the existing estimates of the contribution of education to an economy's productivity, however, has little to say about how new technologies are generated and adopted or about their interaction with education. This is mainly caused by two assumptions of neoclassical economics: One is the prevalence of equilibrium conditions, the other is that market conditions determine economic outcomes. Neoclassical economics, like every other theoretical framework, provides a particular focus and this necessarily obscures other aspects.

The assumption that the economy and individual industries are in equilibrium (which may be a moving equilibrium) prevents an analysis of disequilibrium phenomena such as the diffusion of innovations, the growth and decline of individual firms, and changes in the value of specific knowledge and education. But in the economics of technological change, it has long been argued that dynamic processes like innovation (which cannot coexist with competitive equilibrium) play a major role in technical progress (Schumpeter, 1934, 1942). Nelson and Phelps (1966), Welch (1970), and Schultz (1975) stress the role of education in improving an individual's or a society's ability to cope with disequilibrium situations. In their opinion, technical change opens new opportunities by creating disequilibrium situations, which can be better exploited by a more-educated workforce; faster diffusion of innovations increases the rate of productivity growth. Thus, education and technical change are complements, instead of being independent as in the growth accounting world: The contribution of the allocative effect of education to economic growth is lower in technically stagnant economies or industries than in technically progressive ones.

The second assumption—that market structures determine economic outcomes and that organizations and institutions such as regulatory regimes, ET systems, or labor unions, are irrelevant—is similarly problematic. Chandler (1990) regards the differing organizational capabilities of firms, which depend on their human resources and previous experience, as the main factor that determines the shape of markets. Finegold (1991) and Soskice (1991) demonstrate in equilibrium models how the organization of ET-business links and other institutional factors can affect individual ET efforts and overall levels. Baumol (1990) and Murphy, Shleifer, and Vishny (1991) consider how the allocation of human resources to different occupations affects a country's economic growth. Institutional settings that provide high private returns to "rent seeking" occupations (occupations in which the private returns derive from the redistribution of wealth rather than the creation of new wealth, e.g., divorce lawyers) lead to slower rates of productivity and income growth.

More microeconomic oriented comparisons of British industries with those of other countries indicate that productivity problems are less related to an outdated capital stock than to technically unsophisticated management and workers and an absence of organized knowledge creation through R&D in Britain (Carter and Williams, 1957; Pratten, 1976; Pavitt, 1980; Prais, 1990).

Thus, the estimates presented in Chapters Three and Four may not provide the answers to the question of how investments or changes in the ET sector improve a country's productivity, technological progress, or international competitiveness. This problem goes beyond the issue of ET and concerns productivity growth in general. Nelson (1981), one of the leading researchers in the economics of technological change, has reviewed the research on productivity growth and concludes that "more eclectic or even radically new approaches" are necessary to provide an appropriate analytic framework to these questions central to long-run economic welfare.

A new impetus to analyze the role of ET may come from the heterodox literature in the history of economic development and the economics of technological change. Two theoretical frameworks play a prominent role in this literature: transaction cost theory and evolutionary economic theory. The transaction cost theory, developed by Williamson (1975, 1985), focuses on the role of imperfect information in transactions, suggesting that firms develop in an attempt to minimize the costs of production and transactions; evolutionary economic theory (Nelson and Winter, 1982) focuses on the development of the economy as individual firms grow and decline. Both approaches are more systems-oriented than the prevalent neoclassical approach, discussed in Chapters Three and Four.[1] Similar to the dichotomy between the microeconomic returns-to-education and the macroeconomic growth accounting literature, the next two sections consider ideas pertinent to the individual firm and to the development of an industry or economy.

THE BUSINESS FIRM AS THE UNIT OF ANALYSIS

Firms are the driving force behind technical change and should be at the center of an analysis of the interaction between ET and technical progress. Clearly, the success or failure of a firm ultimately depends on management and employees. A better-educated and trained workforce can be profitable for a firm if it results in a higher level of innovation and if competitors are not able to imitate these improvements; alternatively, a more qualified workforce may be profitable if it enables a firm to imitate a competitor's innovation quickly. The importance of human resources on a firm's success has been touted in much of the popular business literature (Peters and Waterman, 1982; Schuster, 1986) and also has its own subfield in the management literature (Beer et al., 1985; Byers and Rue, 1987; Pieper, 1990). Unfortunately, as the reviews by Vroom (1976) and Hackman and Oldham (1980) show, research has not yet revealed robust relationships between variables under management control and an organization's effectiveness or productivity. In some specific cases, a

---

[1]The exception are the principal-agent models that can explain why it is efficient for a firm to separate wages from the current productivity of a worker. Information asymmetries are a central feature in both the principal-agent and the transaction cost theory.

positive relationship between educational achievement and new technology has been established (Coleman, Katz, and Menzel, 1957; Welch, 1970; Bartel and Lichtenberg, 1987), but the overall evidence is sketchy.

Chandler (1977, 1990) sees business firms as the key players shaping markets, economic development, and the competitiveness of nations. The dynamic force for the growth of individual firms derives from their organizational capabilities, which are created during the knowledge-acquiring processes of commercializing new products. These capabilities depend on the skills of individuals, which in turn are developed by the organizational setting in which they are used. Over the long run, a firm-specific hierarchy of organizational routines develops, defining the activities that the firm can perform confidently. The creation of such an organizational base can be explained by the transaction cost theory. Chandler discusses the success of German chemical firms over British entrepreneurs, who had almost every advantage around 1870. In addition to building large plants to take advantage of economies of size and scope, the Germans created a worldwide sales force of trained chemists to teach customers how to apply new products, whereas the British continued to rely on independent middlemen to distribute their products.

It is not surprising that economic studies of technological change show that differences in productivity growth across firms and industries can be explained to a substantial part by R&D spending (Nelson and Winter, 1977). Firms experiencing rapid technological advance tend to invest heavily in R&D or receive their inputs from firms in R&D-intensive industries. The connection between R&D and ET may be closer than it appears at first sight: Cohen and Levinthal (1989) argue that firms often perform R&D to improve their ability to evaluate options created by innovations and technical advance outside the firm, rather than to produce proprietary techniques or products. Thus, R&D expenditures measure to a large extent "training" costs for the research staff. The training aspect of R&D is probably the dominating reason why firms perform basic research with their own money (Rosenberg, 1990; Pavitt, 1991). Gambardella's (1993) case studies of U.S. pharmaceutical companies offer the empirical evidence that in-house scientific research raises the ability of firms to take advantage of "public" science. These conscious learning activities do not simply make a firm more productive, but they enhance a firm's technological knowledge and capabilities, opening up a new range of trajectories of technological advance (Malerba, 1992). Some researchers believe that cutbacks in industrial R&D expenditures are one reason why the U.S. technological lead over Germany and Japan has eroded (Hayes and Abernathy, 1980). Industrial capabilities to take advantage of outside scientific developments declined to the extent that "cost saving" measures, primarily aimed at the perceived luxuries of in-house basic research, reduced training for researchers.

Although the focus on firms and knowledge in the literature of technological change is a promising alternative to the focus on individuals in isolation as in the human capital literature, research so far has largely been limited to the most educated part of the workforce and has not considered the much larger group of workers without college education. An important exception are several European studies that compare the effect of ET across all employee groups at the firm level by comparing the organization of matched firms across countries (Daly et al., 1985; Steedman and Wagner, 1987, 1989; Prais et al., 1989; Prais, 1990; Mason et al., 1992). Most of these studies compared Britain and Germany and found German firms to be more productive across a variety of manufacturing sectors. German firms performed better because German workers had greater capability to maintain machinery and operate more sophisticated equipment. The authors ascribed this to a stronger vocational training system and to foremen with advanced technical skills. A similar productivity lag appeared in services, where German hotels had lower labor requirements per guest night than comparable British hotels. Prais et al. (1989) credited vocational training and higher professional standards in Germany for this productivity advantage. The main difference between Germany and Britain was a larger fraction of qualified manpower in Germany, which even increased the productivity of unqualified employees, such as chambermaids, through better organized work processes.

Using a more standard economic production function approach, Bartel (1991) has studied the effect of company training programs on firm productivity quantitatively. Instead of analyzing wages or the productivity of individuals, she has estimated a firm's productivity using data on personnel policies and economic characteristics of manufacturing firms. Her dataset is taken from a 1986 Columbia Business School survey of 495 business lines.[2] Changes in personnel policies are assumed to change the relationship between reported labor (number of employees) and "effective" labor, which is one component in the production function, and this effect can be estimated. Her main findings are that businesses that were operating below their expected labor productivity levels implemented new employee training programs; these programs resulted in significantly larger increases of labor productivity growth. New personnel policies other than training did not have significant effects on productivity growth, thus establishing a relationship between training and labor productivity at the organizational level.

EVOLUTIONARY ECONOMICS

Although the study of individual firms can provide a better understanding of how educational policies affect productivity at the firm level than the returns-to-education framework, it is necessary to have a broader framework to aggregate firm histories to the economy level. Nelson and Winter (1982) have been among the main proponents of an evolutionary theory of productivity growth, although many of the ideas are shared by economic historians and economists of technological change (Chandler, 1990; David, 1993; Mowery and Rosenberg, 1989; Rosenberg, 1982). The complexities of internal firm organization or the effects of specific types of training are not specifically considered, but the basic framework is consistent with the facts of technological change at the industry level.

An economy grows as new products and techniques are invented and used over time. But firms and industries are not progressing equally and the ones that successfully develop new techniques or products grow at the expense of less-productive ones. If high-quality staff improves a firm's chances of succeeding, this may provide a different explanation of changing educational levels in the labor force caused by innovation and technical progress than the ones suggested in the deskilling controversy, which considers only technically imposed job requirements. Thus, testing the relevance of the implications of the

---

[2]A business line corresponds to a division for large companies operating in several distinct areas; otherwise, a business line is the same as a company.

evolutionary view could be a substantial contribution to the literature on education and productivity.

So far, most of the research in this paradigm has focused on the relationship between formal knowledge creation through R&D and technological change, although empirical investigations have been relatively scarce compared to the human capital literature. This is to some extent caused by a lack of longitudinal data on individual firms. For obvious reasons, existing datasets have little information on a firm's labor force or outputs and even less on costs, profits, or R&D, often considered to be a strategic variable. Nevertheless, empirical research has revealed a number of surprising regularities. These regularities may have important implications for the role of ET as well, especially considering the role that R&D plays in training employees to take advantage of outside knowledge. The best-known empirical studies are Mansfield (1968) and Griliches (1984); Cohen and Levin (1989) provide a recent review.

One phenomenon is the positive cross-sectional correlation between R&D intensity and industry concentration. Although it has initially been argued that market concentration leads to higher R&D spending, the more recent view considers them to be simultaneously determined. Does a similar relationship hold between educational and training levels of an industry's workforce, market concentration, and innovation?

Another positive relationship has been found between R&D expenditures and productivity growth. Of course, researchers have argued that the fairly stable rank-ordering of industries (chemical, petroleum, and electrical machinery are among the most research intensive industries) could be attributable to technological opportunities. But "technological opportunity" also implies quickly changing economic opportunities, which according to the allocative effect of education would lead to higher returns to education in these sectors, another testable hypothesis.

Finally, the average productivity of R&D, measured in terms of patents or innovation per dollar, tends to be lower for larger firms, although absolute R&D expenditures grow with firm size. In general, this is interpreted as a disadvantage for larger firms. But there could be a different explanation: A small innovation can have a higher payoff in a larger firm simply because it affects more people or products. Thus, larger firms may be more willing to sponsor marginal projects than smaller firms. A similar relationship is likely to hold for human resources. Better management skills have a higher payoff in large companies, a hypothesis that is consistent with the fact that managers in large companies tend to receive higher salaries than managers in small firms.

Chapter Six

CONCLUSIONS

This survey has reviewed research on the role of education and training for economic performance. Because policy debates are often shaped by a fairly myopic view of economic conditions—and the discussions of the ET are no exception—an important part of this report provided a more long-run and international perspective of economic trends and education. Other countries, in particular Japan and the countries of Western Europe, are not quickly surpassing the United States, but are rather approaching the U.S. level of per capita GDP and labor productivity. This convergence was possible because these countries improved their social capability (and education is an important element) to exploit the "advantages of backwardness." The U.S. share of manufacturing output in the OECD, like Japan's, has not declined because of a lack of "competitiveness" but has increased, whereas the share of Germany and of other OECD countries dropped. Although the U.S. share of OECD exports has become smaller overall, high-technology industries fared relatively better.

Most economic research directly concerned with ET can be grouped into two approaches—one focusing on the macroeconomic phenomenon of economic growth, the other one analyzing the effect of ET on individual wages and (to a lesser extent) worker productivity. But the intellectual framework underlying these approaches is not well suited to analyze the current policy issues of international competitiveness and technological change. Some promising alternatives in the economics of technological change take a more systems-oriented approach, although they have yet to be applied to ET. An important exception are the matched firm comparisons by Prais and his collaborators. This approach is currently extended to the United States in joint research with RAND.

The main shortcoming of the growth accounting approach, which tries to divide up the credit for economic growth, is the assumption that the sources of growth are independent. Changes in the ET system, technological change, or investment in physical capital are taken as exogenously determined, even though there are good reasons to believe that there are strong interdependencies between these factors. In addition, the measurement of ET is incomplete and largely limited to years of formal education. An unsolved puzzle is the large variation across countries in the estimated role of education in economic growth. An investigation of the cause of this variance could provide major new insights into the macroeconomic role of ET. For example, it was found in Chapter Three that the contribution of labor quality improvements to growth was very small in Germany but TFP growth was high. Was part of the German TFP growth caused by training and other nonformal education excluded from standard growth accounting calculations?

The microstudies of the effect of ET on productivity also employ assumptions that may limit their usefulness for policy guidance in a changing environment. ET is assumed to raise skills, making individuals more productive, but the literature is silent about dynamic changes in the economy: The human capital studies assume a static economy in equilibrium even though economic growth is characterized by disequilibrium situations. The only exception are a few papers that extended the static "worker" effect of ET to include a dynamic "allocative" effect. The inadequate formulation of the social rates of returns to education, a central issue for efficient educational planning, is closely related. Current estimates are based on individual earnings and ignore economic externalities, which occur both in a static environment (if an individual's education improves the welfare of others) and in a dynamic context (if education generates new economic opportunities in the future).

The final chapter discusses alternative approaches that can address several of the central features of economic growth that have been ignored in the existing economic literature on ET's contribution to productivity. Although there is no general framework to estimate the role of ET in an economy yet, the discussion suggests a number of hypotheses that can be explored: Are ET levels higher in concentrated industries? Are industries with higher ET levels experiencing faster productivity growth? Are ET levels related to firm size? There is much to be learned from considering the role of ET in a similar framework as the role of R&D. At the same time, this may provide new insights into technological change.

BIBLIOGRAPHY

Abramowitz, M., "Welfare Quandaries and Productivity Concerns," *American Economic Review*, 71(1), March 1981, pp. 1–17.

Abramowitz, M., "Catching Up, Forging Ahead, and Falling Behind," *Journal of Economic History*, 46, June 1986, pp. 385–406.

Abramowitz, M., *Thinking About Growth*, Cambridge University Press, 1989, Cambridge, England.

Adams, J. D., "Fundamental Stocks of Knowledge and Productivity Growth," *Journal of Political Economy*, 98(4), 1990, pp. 673–702.

Altonji, J. G., and J. R. Spletzer, "Worker Characteristics, Job Characteristics, and the Receipt of On-the-Job Training," *Industrial and Labor Relations Review*, 45, October 1991, pp. 58–79.

Altonji, J. G., "The Effects of High School Curriculum on Education and Labor Market Outcomes," NBER Working Paper 4142, August 1992.

Arrow, K. J., "The Economic Implications of Learning by Doing," *Review of Economic Studies*, 29, June 1962, pp. 155–173.

Arrow, Kenneth, "Higher Education as a Filter," *Journal of Public Economics*, 2, 1973, pp. 193–216.

Ashenfelter, O., "Estimating the Effect of Training Programs on Earnings," *Review of Economics and Statistics*, 60, February 1978, pp. 47–57.

Ashenfelter, O., and D. Card, "Using the Longitudinal Structure of Earnings to Estimate the Effect of Training Programs," *Review of Economics and Statistics*, 67(4), November 1985, pp. 648–660.

Attewell, P., "The De-Skilling Controversy," *Work and Occupations*, 14(3), August 1987, pp. 323–346.

Attewell, P., "What Is Skill?" *Work and Occupations*, 17(4), November 1990, pp. 422–448.

Bailey, M. N., and R. J. Gordon, "The Productivity Slowdown in the Service Sector: Can It Be Explained by Measurement Errors?" *The Service Economy*, 2(4), 1988.

Barro, R. J., "Economic Growth in a Cross-Section of Countries," *Quarterly Journal of Economics*, 106, May 1991, pp. 407–443.

Barro, R. J., and X. Sala-i-Martin, "Convergence," *Journal of Political Economy*, 100, April 1992, pp. 223–251.

Barron, J. M., D. A. Black, and M. A. Loewenstein, "Employer Size: The Implications for Search, Training, Capital Investment, Starting Wages, and Wage Growth," *Journal of Labor Economics*, 5(1), January 1987, pp. 76–89.

Barron, J. M, D. A. Black, and M. A. Loewenstein, "Job Matching and On-the-Job Training," *Journal of Labor Economics*, 7(1), 1989, pp. 1–19.

Bartel, A. P., and F. R. Lichtenberg, "The Comparative Advantage of Educated Workers in Implementing New Technology," *Review of Economics and Statistics*, 69(1), February 1987, pp. 1–11.

Bartel, A. P., "Formal Employee Training Programs and Their Impact on Labor Productivity: Evidence from a Human Resource Survey," NBER Working Paper 3026, 1989.

Bartel, A. P., "Productivity Gains from the Implementation of Employee Training Programs," NBER Working Paper 3893, November 1991.

Bartel, A. P., "Training, Wage Growth and Job Performance: Evidence from a Company Database," NBER Working Paper 4027, March 1992.

Bassi, L. J., "The Effect of CETA on the Postprogram Earnings of Participants," *Journal of Human Resources*, Fall 1983, pp. 539–556.

Baumol, W. J., and K. McLennan, *Productivity Growth and U.S. Competitiveness*, Oxford University Press, New York, 1985.

Baumol, W. J., S. A. Blackman, and E. N. Wolff, "Unbalanced Growth Revisited: Asymptotic Stagnancy and New Evidence," *American Economic Review*, 75, September 1985, pp. 806–817.

Baumol, W. J., "Productivity Growth, Convergence, and Welfare: What the Long-Run Data Show," *American Economic Review*, 76, December 1986, pp. 1072–1085.

Baumol, W. J., S. A. Blackman, and E.N. Wolff, *Productivity and American Leadership*, MIT Press, Cambridge, Massachusetts, 1989.

Baumol, W. J., and E. N. Wolff, "Three Fundamental Productivity Concepts: Principles and Measurement," in G. Feiwel (ed.), *Joan Robinson and Modern Economic Theory*, Macmillan, London, 1989, pp. 638–659.

Baumol, W. J., "Entrepreneurship: Productive, Unproductive, and Destructive, *Journal of Political Economy*, 98, 1990, pp. 893–921.

Becker, G. S., "Investment in Human Capital: A Theoretical Analysis," *Journal of Political Economy*, 10, October 1962, pp. 9–49.

Becker, G. S., *Human Capital*, Columbia University Press, New York, 1964.

Becker, G. S., *Human Capital*, Columbia University Press, New York, 2nd edition, 1975.

Becker, G. S., and G. J. Stigler, "Law Enforcement, Malfeasance and Compensation of Enforcers," *Journal of Legal Studies*, 3(1), January 1974, pp. 1–18.

Beer, M., B. Spector, P. R. Lawrence, D. Q. Mills, and R. E. Walton, *Human Resource Management*, New York, 1985.

Berg, I., *Education and Jobs: The Great Training Robbery*, Praeger, New York, 1970.

Berndt, E. R., C. J. Morrison, and L. S. Rosenblum, "High-Tech Capital Formation and Labor Composition in U.S. Manufacturing Industries: An Exploratory Analysis," NBER Working Paper 4010, 1992.

Bishop, J. H., "Is the Test Score Decline Responsible for the Productivity Growth Decline?" *American Economic Review*, March 1989, pp. 178–197.

Bishop, J. H., "The Impact of Previous Training in Schools and on Jobs on Productivity, Required OJT, and Turnover of New Hires," Working Paper 91-27, Center for Advanced Human Resource Studies, Cornell University, 1991.

Blanchflower, D., and L. M. Lynch, "Training at Work: A Comparison of U.S. and British Youths," NBER Working Paper 4037, March 1992.

Blaug, M., "The Empirical Status of Human Capital Theory: A Slightly Jaundiced Survey," *Journal of Economic Literature*, 14, 1976, pp. 827–855.

Blaug, M., "Where Are We Now in the Economics of Education?" *Economics of Education Review*, 4(1), 1985, pp. 17–28.

Blaug, M., "Review of Economics of Education: Research and Studies," *Journal of Human Resources*, 24(2), 1989, pp. 331–333.

Bloch, F. E. (ed.), *Evaluating Manpower Training Program*, JAI Press, Greenwich, Connecticut, 1979.

Bound, J., and G. Johnson, "Changes in the Structure of Wages in the 1980's: An Evaluation of Alternative Explanations," *American Economic Review*, 82(3), June 1992, pp. 371–392.

Bowles, S., and H. Gintis, *Schooling in Capitalist America*, Basic Books, New York, 1976.

Braverman, H. *Labor and Monopoly Capital*, Monthly Review Press, New York, 1974.

Bretz, R. D., Jr., "College Grade Point Average as a Predictor of Adult Success: A Meta-Analytic Review and Some Additional Evidence," *Public Personnel Management*, 18(1), 1989, pp. 11–22.

Brown, J. N., "Why Do Wages Increase with Tenure?" *American Economic Review*, 79, December 1989, pp. 971–991.

Byers, L. L., and L. W. Rue, *Human Resource Management*, 2nd edition, Homewood, Illinois, 1987.

Cappelli, P., "College and the Workplace: How Should We Assess Student Performance," Draft in Circulation, November 1991a.

Cappelli, P., "Are Skill Requirements Rising? Evidence from Production and Clerical Jobs," Draft in Circulation, November 1991b.

Carter, C. F., and B. R. Williams, *Industry and Technical Progress*, Oxford University Press, New York, 1957.

Chandler, A. D., *The Visible Hand: The Managerial Revolution in American Business*, Harvard, Cambridge, Massachusetts, 1977.

Chandler, A. D., *Scale and Scope: The Dynamic of Industrial Capitalism*, Harvard, Cambridge, Massachusetts, 1990.

Chari, V. V., and H. Hopenhayn, "Vintage Human Capital, Growth, and the Diffusion of New Technology," *Journal of Political Economy*, 99(6), pp. 1142–1165.

Chinloy, P., "Sources of Quality Change in Labor Input," *American Economic Review*, 70(1), March 1980, pp. 109–119.

Cohen, W. M., and D. A. Levinthal "Innovation and Learning: The Two Faces of R&D," *Economic Journal*, 99, September 1989, pp. 569–596.

Cohen, W. M., and R. C. Levin, "Empirical Studies of Innovation and Market Structure," in R. Schmalensee and R. Willig (eds.), *Handbook of Industrial Organization*, North Holland, Amsterdam, 1989, pp. 1059–1107.

Coleman, J., E. Katz, and H. Menzel, "The Diffusion of an Innovation Among Physicians," *Sociometry*, 20, December 1957, pp. 253–270.

Commission on the Skills of the American Workforce, *America's Choice: High Skills or Low Wages*, National Center on Education and the Economy, Rochester, New York, 1990.

Daly, A., D.M.W. N. Hitchens, and K. Wagner, "Productivity, Machinery and Skills in a Sample of British and German Manufacturing Plants," *National Institute Economic Review*, February 1985, pp. 48–63.

Darby, M., "The U.S. Productivity Slowdown: A Case of Statistical Myopia," *American Economic Review*, 74, June 1984, pp. 301–322.

David, P. A., "Computer and Dynamo: The Modern Productivity Paradox in a Not-Too-Distant Mirror, " in *Technology and Productivity: The Challenge for Economic Policy*, OECD, 1991, pp. 315–348.

David, P. A., "Path-Dependence: Putting the Past into the Future of Economics," *Journal of Economic Literature*, forthcoming, 1993.

Dean, E. (ed.), *Education and Economic Productivity*, Ballinger, Cambridge, Massachusetts, 1984.

Denison, Edward F., *The Sources of Economic Growth in the United States*, Committee for Economic Development, New York, 1962.

Denison, E. F., *Why Growth Rates Differ*, Brookings Institution, Washington, D.C., 1967.

Denison, E. F., *Accounting for United States Economic Growth, 1929-1969*, Brookings Institution, Washington, D.C., 1974.

Denison, E. F., *Accounting for Slower Economic Growth: The United States in the 1970s*, Brookings Institution, Washington, D.C., 1979.

Denison, E. F., "The Contribution of Capital to Economic Growth," *American Economic Review*, 70(2), 1980, pp. 220–224.

Denison, Edward F., "The Interruption of Productivity Growth in the United States," *Economic Journal*, 93, 1983, pp. 56–77.

Dertouzos, M., R. K. Lester, R. M. Solow, and the MIT Commission on Industrial Productivity, *Made in America*, MIT Press, Cambridge, Massachusetts, 1989.

Dickinson, K., T. Johnson, and R. West, "An Analysis of the Impact of CETA Programs on Participants' Earnings," Final Report, SRI International, Menlo Park, California, 1984.

Dollar, D., and E. N. Wolff, "Convergence of Industry Labor Productivity Among Advanced Economies, 1963–1982," *Review of Economics and Statistics,* 70(4), November 1988, pp. 549–558.

Dollar, D. and E. N. Wolff, *Competitiveness, Convergence, and International Specialization,* MIT Press, Cambridge, Massachusetts, 1993.

Dore, R. P., *The Diploma Disease,* Allen & Unwin, London, 1976.

Dore, R. P., and J. Oxenham, "Educational Reform and Selection for Employment—An Overview," in J. Oxenham (ed.), *Education versus Qualification,* Allen & Unwin, London, 1984, pp. 3–40.

Dosi, G., "Sources, Procedures, and Microeconomic Effects of Innovation," *Journal of Economic Literature,* 26(3), September 1988, pp. 1120–1171.

Dosi, G., K. Pavitt, and L. Soete, *The Economics of Technological Change and International Trade,* Wheatsheaf, Brighton, England, 1990.

Duncan, G. J., and S. Hoffman, "On-the-Job Training and Earnings Differences by Race and Sex," *Review of Economics and Statistics,* 61, November 1979, pp. 594–603.

Dye, D. A., and M. Reck, "College Grade Point Average as a Predictor of Adult Success: A Reply," *Public Personnel Management,* 18(2), 1989, pp. 235–241.

Eatwell, J., M. Milgate, P. Newman, *The New Palgrave, A Dictionary of Economics,* Stockton Press, New York, 1987.

Finegold, D., and D. Soskice, "The Failure of British Training: Analysis and Prescription," *Oxford Review of Economic Policy,* 4(3), 1988, pp. 21–53.

Finegold, D., "Institutional Incentives and Skills Creation: Understanding the Skills Investment Decision," in P. Ryan (ed.), *International Comparisons of Vocational Education and Training for Intermediate Skills,* Falmer, London, 1991, pp. 93–118.

Finegold, D., *The Low-Skill Equilibrium: An Institutional Analysis of Britain's Education and Training Failure*, Pembroke College, Oxford, England, 1992.

Finegold, D., L. McFarland, W. Richardson (eds.), *Something Borrowed, Something Blue? A Study of the Thatcher Government's Appropriation of American Education and Training Policy*, Triangle Books, Oxford, England, 1993.

Fonda, N., and C. Hayes, "Education, Training and Business Performance," *Oxford Review of Economic Policy*, 4(3), 1988, pp. 108–119.

Freeman, C., J. Clark, and L. Soete, *Unemployment and Technical Innovation*, Francis Pinter, London, 1982.

Freeman, R., *The Market for College-Trained Manpower*, Harvard University Press, Cambridge, Massachusetts, 1971.

Freeman, R., *The Overeducated American*, Academic Press, New York, 1976.

Gambardella, A., *Science and Innovation in the U.S. Pharmaceutical Industry*, Cambridge University Press, Cambridge, England, 1993.

Gerschenkron, A., *Economic Backwardness in Historical Perspective*, Harvard University Press, Cambridge, Massachusetts, 1962.

Gill, C., *Work, Unemployment and the New Technology*, Basil Blackwell, Oxford, England, 1985.

Godfrey, M., "Education, Training, Productivity and Income: A Kenyan Case Study," *Comparative Education Review*, 21(1), 1977, pp. 29–35.

Gospel, H. (ed.), *Industrial Training and Technological Innovation*, Routledge, London, 1991.

Greenwood, M. J., and J. M. McDowell, "The Factor Market Consequences of U.S. Immigration," *Journal of Economic Literature*, 24(4), 1986, pp. 1738–1772.

Griliches, Z., "Research Expenditure, Education, and the Aggregate Agricultural Production Function, *American Economic Review*, 54, 1964, pp. 961–974.

Griliches, Z., "Capital-Skill Complementarity," *The Review of Economics and Statistics*, 51:4, November 1969, pp. 465–468.

Griliches, Z., "Estimating the Returns to Schooling: Some Econometric Problems," *Econometrica*, 45(1), 1977, pp. 1–22.

Griliches, Z., "Issues in Assessing the Contribution of Research and Development to Productivity Growth," *Bell Journal of Economics*, 10(1), Spring 1979, pp. 92–116.

Griliches, Z. (ed.), *R&D, Patents, and Productivity*, Chicago University Press, Chicago, Illinois, 1984.

Grossman, G. M., and E. Helpman, *Innovation and Growth in the Global Economy*, MIT Press, Cambridge, Massachusetts, 1991.

Hackman, J. R., and G. R. Oldham, *Work Redesign*, Addison-Wesley, Reading, Massachusetts, 1980.

Hanoch, G., "An Economic Analysis of Earning and Schooling," *Journal of Human Resources*, 2, 1967, pp. 310–329.

Hanushek, E. A., "The Economics of Schooling," *Journal of Economic Literature*, 24(3), September 1986, pp. 1141–1177.

Harris, M., and B. Holmstrom, "A Theory of Wage Dynamics," *Review of Economic Studies*, 49(3), July 1982, pp. 315–333.

Hart, P. E., and A. Shipman, "The Variation of Productivity Within British and German Industries," *The Journal of Industrial Economics*, 40(4), December 1992, pp. 417–425.

Haskel, J., and C. Martin, "Do Skill Shortages Reduce Productivity? Theory and Evidence from the United Kingdom," *Economic Journal*, 103, March 1993, pp. 386–394.

Hayes R. H., and W. J. Abernathy, "Managing Our Way to Economic Decline," *Harvard Business Review*, 54(4), July/August 1980, pp. 67–77.

Helliwell, J. F., P. Sturm, and G. Salou, "International Comparisons and the Sources of Productivity Slowdown," *European Economic Review*, 28, 1985, pp. 157–191.

Hirsh, R., *Technology and Transformation in the American Electric Utility Industry*, Cambridge University Press, Cambridge, England, 1989.

Holzer, H., "The Determinants of Employee Productivity and Earnings," *Industrial Relations*, 29(3), 1990, pp. 403–422.

Horowitz, Stanley, and Allen Sherman, "A Direct Measure of the Relationship between Human Capital and Productivity," *Journal of Human Resources*, 15, 1980, pp. 67–76.

Howard, A., "College Experiences and Managerial Performance," *Journal of Applied Psychology*, 71, 1986, pp. 530–552.

International Labor Organization, *The Paper Qualification Syndrome and Unemployment of School Leavers*, Vols. 1 and 2, Jobs and Skills Program for Africa, Addis Ababa, 1981.

International Labor Organization, *Paper Qualification Syndrome and Unemployment of School Leavers, a Comparative Subregional Study*, Jobs and Skills Program for Africa, Addis Ababa, 1982.

Jamison, D. T., and L. J. Lau, *Farmer Education and Farm Efficiency*, Johns Hopkins University Press, Baltimore, Maryland, 1982.

Jorgenson, D. W., and Z. Griliches, "The Explanation of Productivity Change," *Review of Economic Studies*, 34, July 1967, pp. 249–283.

Jorgenson, D. W., "The Contribution of Education to U.S. Economic Growth, 1948-73," in E. Dean (ed.), *Education and Economic Productivity*, Ballinger, Cambridge, Massachusetts, 1984.

Jorgenson, D. W., F. M. Gollop, and B. M. Fraumeni, *Productivity and U.S. Economic Growth*, Harvard University Press, Cambridge, Massachusetts, 1987.

Jorgenson, D. W., and B. Fraumeni, "Investment in Education and U.S. Economic Growth," Discussion Paper 1573, Institute of Economic Research, Harvard University, Cambridge, Massachusetts, 1991.

Jorgenson, D. W., and B. Fraumeni, "The Output of the Education Sector," in Z. Griliches (ed.), *Output Measurement in the Services Sector*, University of Chicago Press, Chicago, Illinois, 1992.

Jovanovic, B., "Job Matching and the Theory of Turnover," *Journal of Political Economy*, 87(5), 1979, pp. 972–990.

Katz, L., and K. Murphy, "Changes in Relative Wages, 1963-1987: Supply and Demand Factors," *Quarterly Journal of Economics*, 107, February 1992, pp. 35–78.

Kazis, Richard, "The Relationship Between Education and Productivity: Implications for the Competitiveness of American Manufacturing and the Movement for Educational Reform," Department of Political Science, Massachusetts Institute of Technology, Cambridge, Massachusetts, 1988.

Kendrick, John W., *Productivity Trends in the United States*, Princeton University Press, Princeton, New Jersey, 1961.

Kendrick, John W., *Postwar Productivity Trends in the United States, 1948-1969*, NBER, New York, 1973.

Kendrick, J., *Understanding Productivity: An Introduction to the Dynamics of Productivity Change*, Johns Hopkins University Press, Baltimore, Maryland, 1977.

Kendrick, J. (ed.), *International Comparisons of Productivity and Causes of the Slowdown*, Ballinger, Cambridge, Massachusetts, 1984.

Krueger, A. B., "How Computers Have Changed the Wage Structure: Evidence from Microdata, 1984-1989," *Quarterly Journal of Economics*, 108, February 1993, pp. 33–60.

Krugman, P. A., "Myths and Realities of U.S. Competitiveness," *Science*, 8, November 1991, pp. 811–815.

Lawrence, R. Z., *Can America Compete?* The Brookings Institution, Washington, D.C., 1984.

Layard, R., and G. Psacharopoulos, "The Screening Hypothesis and the Returns to Education," *Journal of Political Economy*, 82, 1974, pp. 985–998.

Lazear, E., "Academic Achievement and Job Performance," *American Economic Review*, 67, 1977, pp. 252–254.

Lazear E. "Why Is There Mandatory Retirement," *Journal of Political Economy*, 87, 1979, pp. 1261–1284.

Lazonick, W., *Competitive Advantage on the Floor Shop*, Harvard University Press, Cambridge, Massachusetts, 1990.

Lebergott, S., *Manpower in Economic Growth*, McGraw-Hill, New York, 1964.

Lillard, L. A., and H. W. Tan, *Private Sector Training: Who Gets It and What Are Its Effects*, RAND, R-3331-DOL/RC, March, 1986.

Little, A., "Education, Earnings, and Productivity—The Eternal Triangle," in J. Oxenham (ed.), *Education versus Qualification*, Allen & Unwin, London, 1984, pp. 87–110.

Lockheed, M. E., D. T. Jamison, L. J. Lau, "Farmer Education and Farm Efficiency: A Survey," *Economic Development and Cultural Change*, 1980, pp. 37–76.

Lynch, L., "Private Sector Training and Its Impact on the Earnings of Young Workers," NBER Working Paper 2872, 1989.

Lynch, L., "Differential Effects of Post-School Training on Early Career Mobility," NBER Working Paper 4034, 1992.

Machlup, F., *The Production and Distribution of Knowledge in the United States*, Princeton University Press, Princeton, New Jersey, 1962.

Maddison, A., "What Is Education For?" *Lloyds Bank Review*, 112, April 1974, pp. 19–30.

Maddison, A., *Phases of Capitalist Development*, Oxford University Press, Oxford, England, 1982.

Maddison, A., "Comparative Analysis of the Productivity Situation in the Advanced Capitalist Countries," in J. Kendrick (ed.), *International Comparisons of Productivity and Causes of the Slowdown*, Ballinger, Cambridge, Massachusetts, 1984, pp. 59–92.

Maddison, A., "Growth and Slowdown in Advanced Capitalist Economies: Techniques of Quantitative Assessment," *Journal of Economic Literature*, 25(2), June 1987, pp. 1649–1689.

Maddison, A., *Dynamic Forces in Capitalist Development*, Oxford University Press, Oxford, England, 1991.

Malerba, F., "Learning by Firms and Incremental Technical Change," *Economic Journal*, 102, July 1992, pp. 845–859.

Mansfield, E., *Industrial Research and Technological Innovation: An Econometric Analysis*, Norton, New York, 1968.

Mansfield, E., "Basic Research and Productivity Increase in Manufacturing," *American Economic Review*, 70(5), December 1980, pp. 863–873.

Mason, G., S. J. Prais, and B. van Ark, "Vocational Education and Productivity in the Netherlands and Britain," *National Institute Economic Review*, May 1992, pp. 45–63.

Mathews, R.C.O., C. H. Feinstein, and J. C. Odling-Smee, *British Economic Growth, 1856-1973*, Stanford University Press, Stanford, California, 1982.

Maurice, M., A. Sorge, and M. Warner, "Societal Differences in Organizing Manufacturing Units: A Comparison of France, West Germany, and Great Britain," *Organization Studies*, 1, 1980, pp. 59–86.

Medow, J., and K. Abraham, "Experience, Performance, and Earnings," *Quarterly Journal of Economics*, 45, 1980, pp. 703–736.

Medow, J., and K. Abraham, "Are Those Paid More Really More Productive?" *Journal of Human Resources*, 41, 1981, pp. 186–216.

Mincer, Jacob, "On-the-Job-Training: Costs, Returns, and Some Implications," *Journal of Political Economy*, 70, October 1962, pp. 50-79.

Mincer, Jacob, *Schooling, Experience, and Earnings*, Columbia University Press, New York, 1974.

Moffitt, R., "Incentive Effects of the U.S. Welfare System: A Review," *Journal of Economic Literature*, 30, March 1992, pp. 1–61.

Mohnen, P., "International R&D Spillovers in Selected OECD Countries," Cahier de recherche du département des sciences économiques de l'UQAM, No. 9208, 1992.

Mowery, D. C., and N. Rosenberg, *Technology and the Pursuit of Economic Growth*, Cambridge University Press, Cambridge, England, 1989.

Mowery, D. C., "The U.S. National Innovation System: Origins and Prospects for Change," *Research Policy*, 21, 1992, pp. 125–144.

Murphy, K. M., A. Shleifer, and R. W. Vishny, "The Allocation of Talent: Implications for Growth," *Quarterly Journal of Economics*, 106, 1991, pp. 503-530.

Murphy, K. M., and F. Welch, "The Structure of Wages," *Quarterly Journal of Economics*, 107, February 1992, pp. 285–326.

Nelson, R., and E. S. Phelps, "Investment in Humans, Technological Diffusion, and Economic Growth," *American Economic Review*, 56(2), 1966, pp. 69–75.

Nelson, R., "Research on Productivity Growth and Differences," *Journal of Economic Literature*, 19, 1981, pp. 1029–1064.

Nelson, R., "The Role of Knowledge in R&D Efficiency," *Quarterly Journal of Economics*, 97(3), 1982, pp. 453–470.

Nelson, R., "US Technological Leadership: Where Did It Come From, and Where Did It Go?" *Research Policy*, 19, 1990, pp. 117–132.

Nelson, R., and S. Winter, "In Search of Useful Theory of Innovation," *Research Policy*, 6, Summer 1977, pp. 36–76.

Nelson, R., and S. Winter, *An Evolutionary Theory of Economic Change*, Harvard University Press, Cambridge, Massachusetts, 1982.

Nelson, R., and G. Wright, "The Rise and Fall of American Technological Leadership: The Postwar Era in Historical Perspective,"

Journal of Economic Literature, 30, December 1992, pp. 1931–1964.

Nickell, S. J., "Wage Structures and Quit Rates," *International Economic Review*, 17, February 1976, pp. 191–203.

Norton, R. D., "Industrial Policy and American Renewal," *Journal of Economic Literature*, 24, March 1986, pp. 1–40.

OECD, *National Accounts, Comptes Nationaux*, OECD, Paris, 1993.

Office of Technology Assessment, *Worker Training: Competing in the New International Economy*, U.S. Government Printing Office, Washington, D.C., 1990.

Ohmae, K., *The Borderless World*, Harper, New York, 1990.

Oxenham, J. (ed.), *Education versus Qualification*, Allen & Unwin, London, England, 1984a.

Oxenham, J., "Employers, Jobs, and Qualifications," in J. Oxenham (ed.) *Education Versus Qualification*, Allen & Unwin, London, England, 1984a, pp. 41–86.

Patel, P., and K. Pavitt, "Is Western Europe Losing the Technological Race?" *Research Policy*, 16(2), 1987, pp. 59–85.

Pavitt, K. (ed.), *Technical Innovation and British Economic Performance*, MacMillan, London, 1980.

Pavitt, K., "What Makes Basic Research Economically Useful?" *Research Policy*, 21, 1991, pp. 109–119.

Peters, T. J., and R. H. Waterman, *In Search of Excellence*, New York, 1982.

Pieper, R. (ed.), *Human Resource Management: An International Comparison*, Waltern de Gruyter, Berlin, 1990.

Piore, M., and C. F. Sabel, *The Second Industrial Divide*, Basic Books, New York, 1984.

Plant, M., and F. Welch, "Measuring the Impact of Education on Productivity," in E. Dean (ed.), *Education and Economic*

Productivity, Ballinger, Cambridge, Massachusetts, 1984, pp. 163–193.

Porter, M., *The Competitive Advantage of Nations*, Free Press, New York, 1990.

Prais, S., *Productivity and Industrial Structure*, Cambridge University Press, Cambridge, England, 1981.

Prais, S. J., V. Jarvis, and K. Wagner, "Productivity and Vocational Skills in Services in Britain and Germany: Hotels," *National Institute Economic Review*, November 1989, pp. 52–73.

Prais, S. (ed.), *Productivity, Education and Training*, NIESR, London, 1990.

Pratten, C. F., *Labor Productivity Differentials Within International Companies*, Cambridge University Press, Cambridge, England, 1976.

Psacharopoulos, G., *Earnings and Education in OECD Countries*, OECD, Paris, 1975.

Psacharopoulos, G., *Higher Education in Developing Countries: A Cost-Benefit Analysis*, World Bank, Washington, D.C., 1980.

Psacharopoulos, G., "Returns to Education: An Updated International Comparison," *Comparative Education Review*, 17, 1981, pp. 321–341.

Psacharopoulos, G., "The Contribution of Education to Economic Growth: International Comparisons," in J. Kendrick (ed.), *International Comparisons of Productivity and Causes of the Slowdown*, Ballinger, Cambridge, Massachusetts, 1984, pp. 335–355.

Psacharopoulos, G., "Returns to Education: A Further International Update and Implication," *Journal of Human Resources*, 20(4), 1985, pp. 583–604.

Psacharopoulos, G., and M. Woodhall, *Education for Development: An Analysis of Investment Choices*, Oxford University Press, New York, 1985.

Psacharopoulos, G. (ed.), *Economics of Education: Research and Studies,* Pergamon Press, Oxford, England, 1987.

Rasell, M. E., and E. Appelbaum, "Investment in Learning: An Assessment of the Economic Return," Report, Investment 21, Washington, D.C., 1992.

Reddy, N. M., and L. Zhao, "International Technology Transfer: A Review," *Research Policy,* 19, 1990, pp. 285–307.

Reich, Robert, *The Work of Nations,* Knopf, New York, 1991.

Riley, J. G., "Testing the Educational Screening Hypothesis," *Journal of Political Economy,* 87, 1979, pp. S227–251.

Romer, P. M., "Increasing Returns and Long-Run Growth," *Journal of Political Economy,* 94, October 1986, pp. 1002–1037.

Romer, P. M., "Endogenous Technological Change," *Journal of Political Economy,* 98(5), 1990, Supplement, pp. S71–S102.

Rosen, S., "Hedonic Prices and Implicit Markets," *Journal of Political Economy,* 82, 1974, pp. 34–55.

Rosenberg, N., *Inside the Black Box: Technology and Economics,* Cambridge University Press, Cambridge, England, 1982.

Rosenberg, N., "Why Do Firms Do Basic Research?" *Research Policy,* 19, 1990, pp. 165–174.

Salter, W.E.G., *Productivity and Technical Change,* 2nd edition, Cambridge University Press, Cambridge, England, 1966.

Schultz, T. P., "Education Investments and Returns," *Handbook of Development Economics,* Vol. 1, North-Holland, Amsterdam, 1988, pp. 543–630.

Schultz, T. W., "Investment in Human Capital," *American Economic Review,* 51, 1961, pp. 1–17.

Schultz, T. W., "Education and Economic Growth," in N. B. Henry (ed.) *Social Forces Influencing American Education,* National Society for the Study of Education, Chicago, 1961, pp. 46–88.

Schultz, T. W., *The Economic Value of Education*, Columbia University Press, New York, 1963.

Schultz, T. W., "The Value of the Ability to Deal with Disequilibria," *Journal of Economic Literature*, 13, September 1975, pp. 827–846.

Schultz, T. W., "A Comment on Education and Economic Growth," in J. Kendrick (ed.), *International Comparisons of Productivity and Causes of the Slowdown*, Ballinger, Cambridge, Massachusetts, 1984, pp. 357–360.

Schumpeter, J. A., *The Theory of Economic Development*, Harvard University Press, Cambridge, Massachusetts, 1934.

Schumpeter, J. A., *Capitalism, Socialism, and Democracy*, Harper, New York, 1942.

Schuster, F. E., *The Schuster Report: The Proven Connection Between People and Profit*, New York, 1986.

Soete, L., and R. Turner, "Technology Diffusion and the Rate of Technical Change," *Economic Journal*, 94, September 1984, pp. 612–623.

Solow, R. M., "A Contribution to the Theory of Economic Growth," *Quarterly Journal of Economics*, 70, 1956, pp. 65–94.

Solow, R. M., "Technical Change and the Aggregate Production Function," *Review of Economics and Statistics*, 39, August 1957, pp. 312–320.

Soskice, D., "Skill Mismatch, Training Systems and Equilibrium Unemployment: A Comparative Institutional Analysis," in F. Padoa Schioppa (ed.), *Mismatch and Labor Mobility*, Cambridge University Press, Cambridge, England, 1991.

Spene, M., "Job Market Signalling," *Quarterly Journal of Economics*, 87, 1973, pp. 355–374.

Steedman, H., and K. Wagner, "A Second Look at Productivity, Machinery and Skills in Britain and Germany," *National Institute Economic Review*, November 1987.

Steedman, H., and K. Wagner, "Productivity, Machinery and Skills: Clothing Manufacture in Britain and Germany," *National Institute Economic Review*, May 1989, pp. 40–54.

Steedman, H., G. Mason, and K. Wagner, "Intermediate Skills in the Workplace," *National Institute Economic Review*, May 1991, pp. 60–76.

Summers, R., and A. Heston, "The Penn World Table (Mark 5)," *Quarterly Journal of Economics*, May 1991, pp. 327–368.

Teece, D. J., "Technology Transfer by Multinational Firms: The Resource Cost of Transferring Technological Know-How," *Economic Journal*, 87, June 1977, pp. 242–261.

Teece, D. J., "Perspectives on Alfred Chandler's Scale and Scope," *Journal of Economic Literature*, 31, March 1993, pp. 199–225.

Tyson, Laura D'Andrea, *Who's Bashing Whom? Trade Conflict in High-Technology Industries*, Institute for International Economics, Washington, D.C., 1992.

U.S. Bureau of the Census, *Statistical Abstract of the United States: 1992* (112th edition), Washington, D.C., 1992.

van Ark, Bart, "Comparative Productivity in British and American Manufacturing," *National Institute Economic Review*, November 1992, pp. 63–74.

Vroom, V., "Leadership," in M. D. Dunette (ed.), *Handbook of Industrial and Organizational Psychology*, Rand McNally, Chicago, Illinois, 1976, pp. 1527–1552.

Wakasugi, R., "Why Are Japanese Firms So Innovative in Engineering Technology?" *Research Policy*, 21, 1992, pp. 1–12.

Weisskopf, T. E., S. Bowles, and D. M. Gordon, "Hearts and Minds: A Social Model of US Productivity Growth," *Brookings Papers of Economic Activity*, 2, 1983, pp. 381–450.

Welch, F., "Education in Production," *Journal of Political Economy*, 78, 1970, pp. 35–59.

Williamson, O. E., *Markets and Hierarchies*, Free Press, New York, 1975.

Williamson, O. E., *The Economic Institutions of Capitalism*, Free Press, New York, 1985.

Willis, R. J., "Wage Determinants: A Survey and Reinterpretation of Human Capital Earnings Functions," *Handbook of Labor Economics*, Vol. 1, North Holland, Amsterdam, 1986, pp. 525–602.

Wise, David A., "Academic Achievement and Job Performance," *American Economic Review*, 65, 1975, pp. 350–366.

Wolff, E. N., *Growth, Accumulation, and Unproductive Activity: An Analysis of the Post-War U.S. Economy*, Cambridge University Press, Cambridge, England, 1987.

Wolff, E. N., "Capital Formation and Productivity Convergence over the Long-Term," *American Economic Review*, 81, 1991, pp. 567–579.